Leaders Wanted:
Making Startup Deals Happen

Leaders Wanted:
Making Startup Deals Happen

Advanced Techniques in
Deal Leadership and Due Diligence
for Early Stage Investors

Hambleton Lord
Christopher Mirabile

www.seraf-investor.com

Table of Contents

Part One

An Investor's Guide to Due Diligence in Early Stage Companies

1. Three Guiding Principles of Due Diligence   3
2. Uneven Pavement Ahead - Key Areas of Risk   11
3. Leadership Wanted - Assessing Leadership Teams   19
4. Knife to a Gunfight - Startup Technology and IP   27
5. If You Build It Will They Come? - Verifying Customer Demand   41
6. Room to Run - Startup Uniqueness and Competition   49
7. What the Market Will Bear - Evaluating Go to Market Strategies   59
8. Big Enough to Be Interesting - Market Size and Opportunity   65
9. Does It Compute - Financials and Funding Strategy   75
10. Penalty Box - Legal Issues for Startups   81
11. Will Anyone Care? - Building an Exit Strategy   87
12. The Fine Print - Deal Terms and Payoff   95
13. Getting on the Same Page - Verifying Goal Alignment   105
14. Learning the Hard Way - Due Diligence Mistakes   113

Part Two

The Art and Science of Deal Leadership

15. The Importance of Deal Leadership   123

16. Short and Savvy - Hallmarks of a Good Deal Process   131

17. One Step at a Time - Overview of Deal Stages   139

18. Many Hands, Light Work - The Team Approach to Processing Deals   151

19. Every Team Needs a Coach - Managing the Deal Process   157

20. "Places, Please!" - Organizing a Deal Team   165

21. Grist For the Mill - Gathering Data for Diligence   173

22. Forks in the Road - The Importance of Interim Checkpoints   181

23. Trust but Verify - The Importance of Reference Checking   189

24. Short and to the Point - Producing a Tight Report   193

25. Good to Go - When You Have Enough to Move Forward   199

26. Let's Make a Deal - Negotiating Terms   205

27. Cutting Bait - When to Walk Away   215

Appendix

- Deep Dive Meeting Notes Template   225
- Due Diligence Report   233
- Due Diligence Checklist   243
- Customer Reference Check Questionnaire   251
- Management Assessment Questionnaire   255

Part One

An Investor's Guide to Due Diligence in Early Stage Companies

Some investors will tell you after spending 60 minutes with an entrepreneur they know in their gut whether to make an investment. They rely on their instincts and sometimes their ability to "pattern match" with successful opportunities and entrepreneurs they worked with in their past. At the other end of the spectrum, there are investors who will spend countless hours digging into every aspect of a startup company. They want to feel 100% confident in their investment decision before they sign the check. Comprehensive due diligence efforts like this usually drag on for months and the extra effort may do relatively little to de-risk the deal.

What is challenging to explain is that both types of investors meet with some success, and both types meet with some failure. Because so much judgment is involved in investing, it can be very hard to know what the right amount of diligence is, and how to go about it. It turns out that picking the right level of diligence is achievable: due diligence is really nothing more than the gathering of additional facts which you can consider before making a decision.

If you need to make a decision, it will generally be easier if you have some data. There is no specific amount necessary, and not all data will be directly helpful with the decision. The amount will vary by stage of company. But good data, timely and efficiently gathered, will never hurt.

Our Approach to Due Diligence

In our roles as Managing Directors at Launchpad Venture Group, we believe in a balanced approach to due diligence. As Christopher likes to say: "We major on the majors." Over the years and after making investments in more than 100 companies, we designed a process that is intended to be quick, efficient and focused on the key issues which underpin the key risks. Executed properly our process can be completed in under 40 aggregate person hours of effort. Split this effort across a team of investors and you have a very fast and manageable project.

Before we dig into how our process is structured, it's important to describe the stage of company we are typically examining. We invest very early in a company's lifespan. Usually, the company is pre-revenue, though in some cases they might have up to $1M in annual revenue. So to be clear, we aren't talking about businesses with substantial operating histories, multiple divisions, multiple geographies, large teams or complex product portfolios. In the parlance of early stage investors, we are looking at companies during their Series Seed or Series A rounds of investment.

This section is filled with many real world examples of what we run into when trying to wrap our arms around a potential new investment. Alongside our "war stories" are practical examples of the tools and techniques we use on a daily basis. We can't thank the members of our angel group, Launchpad, enough. They are instrumental in helping us develop our approach to due diligence and they keep us honest as we continually evolve our methodology. We want to thank them all for their guidance and wisdom!

Chapter 1

Three Guiding Principles of Due Diligence

One of the biggest challenges in doing diligence reviews is knowing when to stop and when to press ahead. The diligence process is a fickle beast - there are times when it takes discipline to keep going in the face of mounting issues, and there are times when it takes discipline to call a time out despite accelerating deal momentum. Diligence is not only about identifying risks, it is about putting those risks in perspective and figuring out which ones matter and which ones don't.

It can be very discouraging to get into a diligence project and begin finding issues and realizing the story is not as complete and attractive as you first thought it was. The desire to quit the effort can be very seductive. Equally seductive is the desire to minimize late-breaking issues once you have put a ton of time and work into a deal. In both cases, allowing yourself to be seduced in the moment can lead to big mistakes. So you need a framework that builds in natural evaluation points or circuit breakers to give you the opportunity to reestablish your perspective and honestly review where you are relative to where you think you should be.

At Launchpad we tackle this with a design that divides the diligence process into three distinct phases, each designed to carry you safely through the seduction zones with the appropriate level of encouragement or realism.

The phases are:

1. Identify Key Risks

2. Develop the Investment Thesis

3. Acknowledge "What Needs to Be Believed" to Invest.

In the first phase, we hold disappointment at bay because we know we are supposed to focus on identifying the key risks. Because we know collecting "warts" is the goal of this phase, the fact that risks and issues and questions are piling up does not feel overly-discouraging. We have the courage to press on (assuming we don't find any huge red flags). This first phase is the fact-gathering phase - we are not trying to pass judgement (except in cases where it is inescapable) - we are just trying to take inventory.

In the second phase, we are trying to sort and prioritize what we learned and see if we can still synthesize a workable investment thesis. Sure, there are issues that need to be run to ground, but does the premise still hold some water? Does it still feel like there is some potential? Can you form a thesis about how you might make money? Here, instead of suspending judgement as in the first phase, we are applying our judgement and our skepticism to figure out whether we still have an opportunity on our hands.

The third phase is where we weave it all together and try to blend both the original optimistic perspective as well as the newly-informed pessimistic perspective. Our challenge is to see if we can boil it down to a simple set of key assumptions or beliefs one would have to hold in order to invest. Some of the assumptions might be positive, such as: "the company will find customers who adopt this despite the higher price," and some of them might be negative, such as: "the final technical hurdles will not pose a serious challenge." But in each case they are the basic assumptions you are going to have to make your peace with if you are going to invest. The beauty of the "belief" phase is that it forces you to be be honest with yourself, take a big picture perspective, and net the whole thing out.

Let's take a closer look at each of the three phases.

Identify Key Risks

After listening to the entrepreneur's presentation, we caucus to discuss first impressions and immediate top of mind questions and concerns. From that we are able to distill it down and pull together a list of 3 or 4 critical areas that need further examination. These areas are usually covered to one degree or another in the investor pitch deck (e.g. customer problem, market opportunity, management team, competition, financials, etc.). Each topic area is naturally going to have a few important questions that we need to further research.

> Diligence team members work together to distill the list of key questions we are really trying to answer and disregard questions which will not add value in a given situation.

For the sake of completeness, we cross-check against our due diligence checklist when forming these questions. But, to keep the process efficient and focused, our diligence team members work together to distill the list of key questions we are really trying to answer and disregard questions which will not add value in a given situation. The answers to the key questions help us identify the areas of solid ground as well as the key risks that will need to be addressed for the company to achieve a successful exit for the investors.

Develop the Investment Thesis

Ultimately when you are forming an investment thesis, you are building a model or likely scenario in your head. An important filter that can help when assessing potential investment opportunities is sometimes defined as the Three P's: Potential, Probability and Period. Formulating the Three P's into questions, we have the following:

- Total Potential of this Company's Success: Is this a billion dollar IPO opportunity or is it more likely to be acquired for under $50M? Or something in between?

- Overall Probability of Success: Are there a limited number of risks that can be mitigated or are we buying a lottery ticket for Powerball?

- Likely Period Until Pay-out: Will it take 10 years to complete the product and get FDA approval, or could this company be acquired in the first couple years by a big competitor?

Acknowledge What Needs to Be Believed

Once we have a handle on the key risks, and we have built an investment thesis, we need to synthesize them into a workable company hypothesis. The best way to keep yourself honest when doing this is to take the trouble to acknowledge and actually list "what needs to be believed" for the investment to make sense. Thus, when we get to the final stage of our due diligence effort, and we write up our very brief report, we make sure we know and prominently document right at the beginning "What Needs to Be Believed" or WNTBB. If an investor just cannot get comfortable that something on the WNTBB will come true, then maybe this deal is not for them.

> When we get to the final stage of our due diligence effort, and we write up our very brief report, we make sure we know and prominently document right at the beginning "What Needs to Be Believed."

The core of the WNTBB exercise is really a test to make sure we are not fooling ourselves. It forces us to ask:

- Have we identified the key risks?

- Do we understand the premise of the deal (i.e. the investment thesis)?

- Is there a balanced logic to the deal?

14 Key Factors of Due Diligence

Now you have a very high level conceptual overview of our Due Diligence Process. To make it fully understandable, and more importantly, something you can actually practice, we need to delve into more detail. In the following chapters of this book, our goal is for you to better understand the types of questions we ask, major risks that concern us, and how we structure our deals to work well for founders and investors. In these chapters, we will take an in depth look at the following:

- **Key Risks**: With early stage companies, what are the key areas of risk every investor needs to accept?

- **Management Team**: Beyond simple reference checks, how do you assess the leadership team?

- **Technology**: What must you understand to determine if a company has breakthrough technology?

- **Product/Solution**: How do you evaluate whether customers really need the company's product?

- **Intellectual Property**: How do you evaluate the importance and strength of the company's Intellectual Property? Have they built any significant barriers to entry with IP or any other means?

- **Go-to-Market Strategy**: Does the company have the right initial strategy for selling to the customer and a plan for doing it at scale?

- **Competition**: What is the competitive environment including but not limited to the set of competitors that the company identifies? What will it be in 5 years?

- **Market Opportunity**: What is the long term potential for the company based on the addressable market opportunity today and in the near future?

- **Financials**: After digging into the financial model do you understand key assumptions and near term milestones for this current round of financing?

- **Funding Strategy**: What is the model for the long term funding strategy of the company and how will different strategies impact the early investors?

- **Legal**: What legal issues are critical for this early stage company in areas such as regulation, contracts, IP and employment?

- **Exits**: What are the exit opportunities for the company? Who will buy this company and why?

- **Deal Terms**: How do the deal terms, funding strategy and exit opportunities combine to produce a reward that justifies the risk of an early stage investment?

- **Alignment**: And finally, how do you make sure that the goals of the investors and the company founders are in alignment?

This is a lot of material to discuss... and to master. I am sure many of you are wondering how it's possible to cover all these questions in a short, concise due diligence effort. Trust us... we've executed this process many times over the years and it works!

Chapter 2

Uneven Pavement Ahead - Key Areas of Risk

Risk is impossible to avoid in business - it is an inherent part, and necessary ingredient, in all successful undertakings. You shouldn't be afraid of risk and allow it to turn you away from great investment opportunities. Instead, you should focus on understanding what critical risks are involved with an early stage company and the degree to which they have been mitigated with resources, smart planning and preparation. Understanding the adequacy of these plans is an important skill to develop for all investors. Risk is not bad; a lack of strategy for dealing with it is. Remember, without risk, there won't be a great reward!

7 Early Stage Investing Risks

Good decisions begin with good information. During due diligence, you will need to gather basic data to assess the adequacy of planning for each of the following areas:

- Technical Risk
- Market Risk
- Team Risk
- Financing Risk
- Regulatory Risk
- Competitive Risk
- Intellectual Property Risk

As part of the assessment process, you will want to determine whether the risk level is low, medium or high for each area. For low risk areas, you shouldn't put in much effort from a due diligence perspective. For medium risk areas, you might need to perform some cursory diligence. It's the high risk areas where you will need to apply significant resources.

Christopher spent much of his career as a software company General Counsel and later as CFO performing due diligence before making acquisitions. And, over the last decade, he has led and worked on dozens of due diligence teams in advance of making investments in a wide variety of startups. His role as a Managing Director at Launchpad provides him with an interesting perch from which to observe how we evaluate and understand risk as part of our due diligence efforts.

> Good decisions begin with good information. As part of the process, you will want to determine whether the risk level is low, medium or high for each area.

Q

Christopher, at Launchpad most of our investments are in technology companies in areas such as software, life sciences, etc. Explain what risks we are looking for when we talk about Technical Risk.

When we talk about technical risk, we are asking "Does the widget exist yet, and if not, is there any chance that it might not be possible to build?" If a software product is in customer hands, even at a V1.0 level, the technical risk is low - it clearly can be built. If you are trying to build a silicon chip that needs to attain very stringent cost and performance benchmarks, or you are trying to get engineered microbes to create a substance at commercially feasible concentrations, and you have not achieved either, then technical risk is high. Technical risk really boils down to a question of whether you have a competitive offering built, or whether you are still trying to build it.

Q

What about Market Risk? What keeps you up at night?

Market risk is also called "market adoption risk" - it is the risk that customers will not want the product. Will the dogs eat the dog food? Market risk is easy to begin to probe at - get some demos of the product into customers' hands - but extremely difficult to accurately assess. For example, if you survey a bunch of customers about something innovative and relevant to them, of course they are all going to say they want it. But...

- At what price?
- At what cost of sales?
- At what level of buying priority?

Market risk is about trying to assess whether there is going to be genuine demand or "pull" from a large enough segment of customers at a reasonable price, with an acceptable cost and length of sales cycle. It's a lot harder than one initially thinks. Many investors have been burned by failing to recognize "false traction" at the beta customer stage. Market risk and market size are closely related - as you go up in customer buying priorities, you generally go down in market size - since more people feel a problem generally than acutely.

> Market risk is about trying to assess whether there is going to be genuine demand or "pull" from a large enough segment of customers at a reasonable price, with an acceptable cost and length of sales cycle.

Q

We like to say that "Team" is the most important factor in whether we choose to invest in a company. What are some of the most important risk factors you look for with the team?

Assuming we are not talking about a team that is incomplete, totally lacking in skills, or has terrible chemistry - you would give a quick "no" in those situations - most team risk comes from the personality, temperament and character of the individuals themselves.

A high functioning team is more than a group of high functioning individuals, but you need to start with high functioning individuals as building blocks. You are looking for people with integrity, tenacity and both book learning and street smarts. And having a CEO with leadership charisma is also crucial. We talk in more detail about these themes in the team discussion, but suffice it to say, if you are alert, you can generally tell when you are in the presence of teams that are not working or are composed of lackluster individuals. Remember, during diligence you are in the honeymoon period - everyone is on their best behavior. If you see even the slightest hint of an issue, it is best to dig in a little further and get to the bottom of it. If there is trouble at this stage, it will get far worse when the stress and pressure of operating a start-up mounts.

Q

Since we are providing the financing for the company, shouldn't we be able to control the financing risks?

No; financing risk is about future financing needs. We can take care of the immediate financing needed to get to the next few key milestones, and likely the next financing round as well, but ...

- How much additional financing will the company likely need?

- Where will that money come from?

- Will it be available on reasonable terms once the company has used up the current round?

- Who are the right investors for this company going forward?

- What will the market be like for financing in 18 months? 36 months?

These are issues we discuss when we talk about financing risk. And the only way to really address it is to know the macro market for financing and the benchmarks applied by those likely to be providing the capital. Then you can build a reasonable plan with the current financing round that has some room for error to get the company to relevant benchmarks for the next round.

A high functioning team is more than a group of high functioning individuals, but you need to start with high functioning individuals as building blocks.

Q

Regulatory risks are not a key factor for many of our investments. But some companies do face these risks. When do we need to understand how the regulatory environment will affect a company?

Not all regulatory situations introduce risk. Sometimes they can provide tailwinds whereby new rules may hasten adoption of a company's solution. But more often they are a form of permission you need to obtain, such as FDA-clearance or other certified vendor or standards-compliant status. These necessary permissions take time and cost money. And they pose the risk that the permission will not be forthcoming. Sometimes they come not from regulatory bodies, but out of the blue from Attorneys General, such as in the case of grey area undertakings like the Fantasy Sports sites, DraftKings and FanDuel.

Understanding what is involved to successfully receive regulatory approval or avoid enforcement scrutiny is critical to understanding the regulatory risk. And then there is always the risk that the regulatory environment might change suddenly and unpredictably in an adverse manner, so it is important to understand the landscape of possible changes.

Q

Every company will have some competition, so this is a risk that I would expect to be a frequently studied issue. What are some of the key issues you like to dig into?

Competition is not a problem per se. A favorite joke of mine is "show me an entrepreneur with no competition and I will show you an entrepreneur with no market." Competitors can help legitimize a product category, bring press coverage and help defray the cost of educating customers. But...

- They can drive up the length of the sales cycle by introducing fear, uncertainty and doubt in the minds of customers with future product announcements.

- They can drive up the cost of sales by creating a lot of noise and counter-selling you have to overcome to be heard.

- They can undermine pricing power and compress margins.

- They can drive you to have to spend more on R&D to stay competitive.

- And, even competitors with a worse solution but access to capital can use brute force marketing and selling techniques to take your market share by sheer effort and saturation techniques.

Understanding competitive risks is about understanding the relative attractiveness, both current and projected into the future, of your company's offering, and understanding who the other players are - both now and in the near future. Other things to consider include:

- Are the competitors all similar-sized peers looking to co-exist in a market large enough for all?

- Or, are they deep pocketed giants who feel that domination of the market is strategically important

and will give away a product if they need to?

- Are there big players in adjacent spaces who could easily jump over into your space once it is validated as an attractive market?

At the end of the day, you want enough running room that you can grow faster than the market and get enough of a strategic toehold. You are trying to carve out space with some enduring value.

> Competitors can help legitimize a product category, bring press coverage and help defray the cost of educating customers.

Q

Last question is on Intellectual Property (IP). What do we look for here?

There are two aspects to the IP analysis. The first is a basic defensive analysis: is there some white space here amongst everyone else's claims? Are we free to even operate at all without infringing someone's intellectual property?

The second is offensive: can we build some IP that allows us to protect our space and block others from competing using our methods?

A third aspect to consider with patents, particularly in crowded spaces, is whether a company can develop some patents that can be used as trading cards or counter-claims in case someone tries to attack the company.

Beyond the basic strategic offensive and defensive questions, you also need to do a tactical review to make sure the company is using 3rd party IP such as open source software and other licensed tools correctly, is perfecting ownership in employee-

created innovations, and has proper controls to protect confidentiality - of the company's information as well as information entrusted to it by partners. A lack of awareness and sophistication about IP can be an important risk factor in diligence.

Chapter 3

Leaders Wanted - Assessing Leadership Teams

Great ideas are a dime a dozen. For example, living in the Boston/Cambridge area, we are surrounded by some of the most innovative researchers in the world working at institutions like MIT and Harvard. I'm pretty confident when I say, in Boston, hardly a day goes by when some graduate student or professor doesn't invent a new product, discover a new molecule or create a cool app. Unfortunately, without a great team behind that new product, it's doubtful that a great company will result.

There is an old saying that goes something like this... "I'd rather invest in an A team with a B plan than a B team with an A plan." Without a doubt, we feel this is the most important point for investors to embrace. Once you understand how critical the team is to a successful outcome, the greater success you will have as an investor. As a long term serial entrepreneur and a successful angel investor, I asked Ham to tell me how he evaluates teams and differentiates the A teams from the B teams.

Q

Ham, let's start with the person at the top. How do you evaluate startup CEOs and what are the most important characteristics you look for?

First and foremost, I look for **integrity**. That character trait might sound obvious and a bit trite, but I feel it's very important to be on alert for trust issues when you are interacting with an entrepreneur. From the initial meeting with the company, during the due diligence

process, and finally while negotiating the deal, I want to make sure the CEO is being honest, straight-forward and genuine. One area that presents a lot of opportunities for problems is the deal negotiation process. It is important to ask whether you are dealing with someone who negotiates in a fair manner. If I sense any duplicity at this early a stage, I can be sure that things will only get worse as the company progresses through the challenges faced by all startups.

From the initial meeting with the company, during the due diligence process, and finally while negotiating the deal, I want to make sure the CEO is being honest, straight-forward and genuine.

That leads me to my second character trait, **tenacity**. It's not easy being a startup CEO. The pressure to succeed is enormous, and CEOs struggle every day to motivate their team. Life in a startup is a series of highs and lows not too dissimilar from riding a roller coaster. One minute life is great as you ship your first product. The next day you hear back from customers that your product is lousy. It takes resilience to handle the good and the bad that a CEO faces on a daily basis. A CEO's tenacity allows her to continue the battle to succeed even when others would give up in despair.

Q

Okay. Those make sense, but there has to be more in the mix than that? What else do you look for?

Next on my list is a combination of **IQ and EQ**. In other words, a CEO needs to be smart and self aware. By "smart", I mean the CEO has the intelligence to discover a major market opportunity, and articulate a plan that will address that opportunity. The CEO has the intelligence to develop high-level strategic plans, and the problem solving skills to deal with day-to-day tactical and execution challenges. By "self aware," I mean the CEO works well with a great team and is willing to take guidance from close advisors. In other words, the CEO must be coachable. A great CEO wants to hire "A" team members who are better than he is for the job being filled.

A CEO with presence has the leadership charisma to command any audience. This type of charisma allows the CEO to take charge whether speaking with employees, customers or investors.

A **deep market understanding** is an important skill set for a CEO because it provides context for the North Star from which the CEO will navigate the company. Great CEOs

21

are two steps ahead of the competition because they have an inherent understanding of where the market is heading.

The final characteristic I look for in a CEO is **presence**. I define presence as follows... A CEO with presence has the leadership charisma to command any audience. This type of charisma allows the CEO to take charge whether speaking with employees, customers or investors. When a CEO with real presence walks into a meeting, people sense it. When they are leading a meeting, you know who is in charge! Furthermore, this ability to command an audience gives the CEO a unique ability to create a winning culture. Building a winning company culture takes constant care and attention from the CEO, and the best way to tend to this task is by communicating a compelling story on a regular basis to the entire company.

Q

Wait - what about experience? What role does experience play in startup success?

This is sort of a trick question. The obvious answer is that experience is critical. You should always back serial entrepreneurs with decades of market experience. Well... that's true in some cases. If you are looking to build the next generation of product or service in a well-established market, having a few grey hairs, knowing the market well and having a deep network of contacts is probably the right way to go.

But, every CEO has to have a first time. And sometimes being a first-timer is actually an advantage. Suppose you are trying to totally disrupt a market or create a new market that has not existed before. For example, you are Jeff Bezos and you are looking to change the way people buy things. When he started Amazon, online retailing was in its infancy. Lots of market experience didn't exist - and much of what did was conventional brick and mortar perspective about how web shopping would never work. Bezos had to make it up as time went on. So disrupting markets takes a very different type of entrepreneur. Success at Amazon had very little to do with experience and much more to do with the ability to try new things and learn as fast as possible!

Q

So you hear the CEO give her pitch and then you spend an hour or two digging into the company to learn more. How are you able to really get to know the CEO and figure out whether she has the key characteristics you are looking for?

The first step that most investors take to learn more about the CEO is to reach out and perform reference checks. Some of the references will be from contacts that the CEO provides to you. Other contacts should be "blind" reference checks with people in your network that know the CEO. This type of background information is useful if you ask the right questions. At Launchpad, we have a well-defined set of questions we use to guide

these interviews. It helps us uncover red flag issues that we need to keep an eye out for, and it helps us apply resources to help the CEO be successful.

Personally, I find the reference checks to be useful but not sufficient in helping me get to know the CEO. I like to take things one step further. In addition to typical due diligence meetings, I arrange for time with the CEO in a non-business setting. For example, I like spending time with the CEO in a public venue outside of an office setting - at a meal or a sporting event - whatever they are comfortable with. Hopefully, our conversation flows smoothly with most of the discussion focused on topics that are not strictly business - past experiences that shaped the person, interests and hobbies, things they like to read, places they would like to travel. This way I get to know the CEO in a different context.

> In addition to typical due diligence meetings, I arrange for time with the CEO in a non-business setting. This way I get to know the CEO in a different context.

Q

Moving beyond the CEO, what skills do you look for in a startup company team?

There are four skills that I look for in a startup team. Given the small size of an early stage company, sometimes these skills are part of the CEO's repertoire, but I like to see them incorporated in the skill set of the other founding members.

- First, I look for **selling** skills. Whether talking to prospects,

investors or future employees, the management team has to be able to sell. If you ain't sellin', nobody's buyin'!

- Second, I look for **technical** skills. I invest in tech companies and so I expect the company will have a great product that will build some competitive barriers to entry. If technical skills are lacking and need to be out-sourced, that can be a real issue for a tech-centric company.

- Third, I look for a deep **market awareness**. As I discussed in one of the above questions, this market awareness is critical for developing the company's strategy.

- Fourth, I look for **product management** skills. This is closely related to market awareness, because it requires the ability to listen to customers and understand the competitive environment. It also requires the ability to translate market needs into a plan that engineering can actually deliver in a timely fashion given limited company resources. Product Management is often an under appreciated skill set. A greater number of tech companies would succeed if they invested more in this critical resource.

And remember, as Christopher pointed out in Chapter 2, a high functioning team is more than a group of high functioning individuals - there has to be good chemistry or intra-personal synergy to tie it all together.

Q

What's the right size for a startup company founding team?

It's not as though there is any magic number here, but I tend to like founding teams with 2 or 3 people. Here's my thinking on why that's the right size. To start with, we won't invest in a company that has only one person involved. There is too much difficulty and that gives rise to too much risk - if a founder can't convince a co-founder to join him in this crazy startup, why would the founder think he can convince investors to put money into the business? With 2 co-founders, the

company is moving in the right direction (read more on Key Founder Issues). Hopefully, the team has complementary skills that help round out the need for the key skills I discussed in the previous question. And, if 2 people can't pull that off, then 3 team members usually can.

Once you move up to founding teams of 4 or more, you are back into the risky zone - you run into a lot of issues with coattail riders, founder dilution, outgrowing the co-founders who aren't producing, etc. Founders often obsess about dilution, and larger teams only make these issues worse.

Q

One final question. What about the fit between the investor(s) and the company?

On a due diligence team, typically, there is one person, in addition to the group manager, who works closely with the CEO throughout the entire due diligence process. At Launchpad, this person is frequently the individual who takes a board seat at the company. It is very important to start building the foundation for a long term relationship between the future board member and the CEO. If this relationship is rocky from the beginning, most likely, it won't survive the stress inherent with early stage companies. So assessing the fit between the presumptive board member and the CEO is a critical step in the due diligence process.

Chapter 4

Knife to a Gunfight - Startup Technology and IP

We all love toys, new ideas, shiny new baubles... Part of the fun of investing in early stage companies relates to the joy we get in trying out new products or imagining how the world will be a better place when a new medical device comes to market. But you have to look beyond the prototype, ignore the flashy product demo, and really dig into the technology before you write that check!

What does it mean to "really dig into the technology"? Are we talking about doing a full code review on a software product? Or, performing a full Freedom To Operate (FTO) review on a medical device company's Intellectual Property (IP)? Some investors would say you need to dig this deep. But there is a huge cost in this level of effort in both time and money. And we can't afford those costs for such early stage investments.

So what is the right balance of effort given our level of investment and stage of company? This is the time where we try to differentiate between:

- A technology which is not yet a product

- A product feature which may never become more than an add-on for someone else's product

- A complete product or product concept that can build a substantial company

And, it's also the time where we need to understand a company's IP ownership. Does the company own the IP or is it owned by a founder or a University? And, are we talking patents or trade secrets when it comes to IP?

Christopher, let's start with the high level technology assessment. How do you determine whether the technology will result in building 1) a substantial company, 2) an add on product, or 3) just another feature?

Humans don't like change. There is a lot of inertia in the familiar and comfortable status quo. To convert users, new products usually need to be significantly better/faster/cheaper than the incumbents. A rule of thumb often cited is that to really galvanize customers and drive adoption, the new product must be clearly and demonstrably 10X better, faster or cheaper than the current state of the art.

And the things that make the product better cannot be subtle things that only a tiny minority of power-users would care about. It has to be a fundamental improvement. A good way to plumb the depths here is to be very alert to discussions of "features." Entrepreneurs love to talk about product features, but it is customer benefits that matter. A good diligence practice is to force the founders to talk only in terms of true customer benefits and then ask yourself if those benefits even remotely approach a 10X improvement for the typical user. If not, you may be a bit short of the mark.

With products in the life sciences it is a little different, but the concept is the same:

- Would this new device, drug, tool or therapy advance the standard of care in a fundamental way?

- Is it good enough that the average users' actual benefits (patient outcomes, practice economics) would be significantly improved?

- Is it enough for the customer to overcome the inertia and risk of abandoning the safe and familiar status quo?

- Would insurers pay for this?

- Would regulators approve of this?

A rule of thumb often cited is that to really galvanize customers and drive adoption, the new product must be clearly and demonstrably 10X better, faster or cheaper than the current state of the art.

Q

Talk to us about Technology Risk. What are we looking for at this early stage in the company's history?

It depends somewhat on the type of product. Due to its intangible nature, software is a lot quicker and easier to fix than hardware with fixed designs and long lead times. But in either case you are looking for a smart overall product architecture that is going to scale well. A great way to test that is to ask how much would need to be re-written in order to handle a 100-fold increase in customer traffic. If it is just a matter of adding additional servers with no material changes to the design, you are probably looking at a scaleable software product. With devices, ask about how hard it would be to cut materials cost in half or what it would cost per unit to build at large scale to uncover key design and knowledge gaps.

An important element of technology risk is the issue of product management. Markets and customer demands evolve constantly. No competitive product can stand still. Successful companies need very strong product management and clear guiding principles. Assessing the strength of the team in this area is essential, and a good way to do that is to have a discussion about the product road map.

- Is there even a roadmap?

- Who wrote and owns it?

- What's on it?

- What was left off?

- Why?

- How far does it go into the future?

- What are some specific examples of things that the team said "no" to upon arriving at this roadmap?

A company that can really hold their own in a detailed product roadmap review has a lot less technical risk than one that cannot.

Q

How important is the technology team? Do you have any issues with technology development being outsourced?

The more tech-centric a company is, the more important it is to have technology skills on the founding team or at least in-house as employees. For a company that is competing on its technology (e.g. software algorithms, bio-sciences, engineering), going to market without strong skills on the team is going to market with missing core competencies. A basketball team that knows how to play basketball will always beat one that needs help from consultants on every play.

> The simple fact of life is that companies with outsourced tech teams get worse "gas mileage" with their funding. They move slower and cost more to run because they have to pay margins to a 3rd party firm.

In situations where technology is a key enabler, but not the absolute basis for competition, it is possible to outsource your technology, using for example, an on- or off-shore software development firm. But when doing diligence on these kinds of situations, great care must be taken to review product roadmaps, assumptions about funding, and speed with which products will reach development milestones.

The simple fact of life is that companies with outsourced tech teams get worse "gas mileage" with their funding. They move slower and cost more to run because they have to pay margins to a 3rd party firm. They have to communicate and coordinate remotely with developers who are not living right there in the trenches and hearing first hand what the customers are saying. This is a problem. It is not an insurmountable disadvantage, but when doing diligence, you must be aware that it is a significant risk and build plans with extra time and money buffers built in. These companies do not implode spectacularly, they bleed to death. They are constantly behind on milestones and keep having to raise more money, each time with a slightly weaker story on progress, until they just cannot raise any more.

Q

With software, it's very common to use open source to accelerate development. What are the issues you need to be aware of with open source?

Incorporating open source software can deliver big time savings and quality enhancements. It is often some of the best tested and most well-understood and actively-developed code around for certain functions. Often it makes very little sense to write from scratch what you could incorporate from a well-respected open source project.

However, just because open source software can be used for free does not mean it does not have restrictions. Open source software is not given away, it is licensed to the user. Even the most mild open source licenses will impose some requirements, such as the requirement to give attribution to the open source project in your software credits. It's no big deal to do this, but if you don't do it, you are in breach of the terms of your license and every IP non-

infringement warranty you give your customers is false.

Some of the licenses on open source projects go much much farther and include terms which embody very strong philosophical viewpoints, such as the notion that all software deserves to be free, and modifiable. These licenses are sometimes referred to as "copyleft" or "viral licenses" in that they impose on the user of the code the requirement that the entire product be licensed on the same terms as the open source component. (The best known examples of these kinds of licenses are the GPL and LGPL licenses.) Unknowingly incorporating code bearing this requirement without the proper packaging care could mean that you are required not only to give your product away for free, but to make the source code available as well.

It is fairly easy to avoid these kinds of license terms, but only if someone who understands the issues is paying attention and tracking the details. If you create a vacuum where engineers who do not have familiarity with these issues were allowed to choose whatever open source code they wanted, based on technical specifications, comfort level or familiarity, without any regard to the licenses involved, you could create an extraordinary mess virtually overnight.

When diligencing these issues, it is very simple to get down to bedrock. You really only need two things:

- A list of every single piece of third party code in the product.

- Assurances from the team that they know the license requirements for each piece of third party code and comply with them.

Any team that cannot pull together such a list, given a reasonable amount of time, is one you should stay very far away from.

Just because open source software can be used for free does not mean it does not have restrictions. Open source software is not given away, it is licensed to the user.

Q

Intellectual Property (IP) can come in many forms. Most people are familiar with patents, and some are aware of trade secrets. What are some of the advantages and disadvantages of each?

This is such a misunderstood subject, that it is worth spending a moment on it. The "big four" - patent, copyright, trademark and trade secret - operate in very

33

different ways because they have entirely different public policy concepts behind them. It is valuable to consider the implications of those differences. Keep in mind that I am talking generally about the US federal statutes. Each state has its own rules, generally very similar and parallel, but not always.

The entire point of **patents** is to encourage the detailed disclosure of novel useful inventions so that they may be used for the good of all humanity. The carrot the government uses to encourage that useful disclosure is the granting of a temporary monopoly on the right to use the concept, usually 20 years. After the temporary monopoly period has expired, anyone can use the patent like a recipe to build copycat technology. Patent law is about getting useful ideas out into the public domain.

Copyright law, on the other hand, is about encouraging creative endeavors by making sure that the authors and creators of things like books, films, software programs, poems, paintings, recordings, sculptures and photographs are able to get paid for their work. Unlike patent coverage, which requires a detailed filing for obvious reasons, copyright protection attaches immediately and automatically as soon as the work is created. Additional protections can be obtained by taking the extra step of registering it with the copyright office, but it is not necessary. If you create something, you have a copyright, and it allows you to prevent others from copying your work unless they agree to terms you set, such as the requirement to pay for your song or for a copy of your software. (Side note: new SaaS models are making this a little trickier - SaaS software is often not licensed but rather access and use is permitted under a services contract.)

> The "big four" - patent, copyright, trademark and trade secret - operate in very different ways because they have entirely different public policy concepts behind them. It is valuable to consider the implications of those differences.

If Patent law is about encouraging disclosure of useful things, and copyright law is about making sure poets and painters can make a living, what is trademark law about? **Trademark** law is a consumer protection statute. It is designed to prevent competitors from offering something of potentially inferior quality that looks confusingly similar to your known and trusted favorite. Federal trademark law says that if you register your logo and the design of your packaging, and it is unique enough to get a trademark, you can prevent anybody from putting a product out there that looks confusingly similar to consumers. That's all. It does not protect the product, but rather just the way it looks in the marketplace.

And what about **trade secret** law? What is the policy goal behind that? Basically, trade secret law is fundamentally industrial policy focused on national competitiveness. Trade secret law is in a lot of ways the most useful and most straightforward of the four forms of IP. The concept is simple: if you have a secret, such as an algorithm, a recipe or a formula, and you derive economic value from its being unknown to your competition, and you take care to keep it a secret, you can prevent anyone who misappropriated it from using it. It is straightforward because it is such a simple concept: if an American company takes money from shareholders and works hard to develop proprietary know-how, and keeps that know-how to itself, no other company from the U.S. or anywhere in the world is allowed to steal that secret and use it to compete in the US market.

In terms of advantages and disadvantages, patents and trademarks require filings, work, and expense to obtain, but offer robust protections in return. Copyright and trade secret do not require any filings and offer the opportunity to monitor and self-police the copying of your work.

OK, so with that said, what are the risks and diligence implications here?

- With **patents**, you want to make sure the patent strategy makes sense: will the the company likely be granted the patents they seek, and will they be of some actual business value (infringement will be discoverable and it will be worth chasing competitors who infringe)? If so, then it is probably worth spending some company money pursuing them. But if the patents are weak, unlikely, hard to monitor, or expensive to enforce, the company may not want to spend as much money or effort chasing the patents.

- With **copyright**, there is not too much that needs to be done except to make sure the company is not plagiarizing the works of others (see open source discussion above), and consider whether the company should register its copyrights. Registering copyrights, in particular valuable works, would give the company access to the U.S. Federal courts and the possibility of treble damages for infringement. (For example, it is possible to obtain a registered copyright for your source code, even with provisions for redacting the bulk of it to keep it a secret.)

- With **trademarks**, you want to make sure the company has done a defensive check to make sure their marks are not stepping on any toes before they build up a lot of brand equity in them in the eyes of customers. And, you want to make sure they take the time to at least seek domestic, if not limited international, protection for the key marks, along with packaging and product collateral.

- With **trade secrets**, you want to make sure the company has tight confidentiality agreements with employees and partners, discloses as little as possible of the sensitive materials, and maintains physical access controls in their facilities where necessary.

Q

In what types of companies are patents critical for building long term value?

Patents are a messy area. At a conceptual level, they have no intrinsic face value - they are merely a right to keep others out of a space. In effect, patents are nothing more than a right to sue to maintain a fence around an area. It is up to the company to make being in that area valuable. If being in the area is valuable, then the right to keep someone out of the area will be valuable.

Where this becomes important is in three basic scenarios:

1. You discover an absolutely key enabler to a breakthrough new technology that allows you to serve a very valuable market in a way no one else can. That is a huge advantage and will result in the patent being valuable.

2. You make and own a key discovery that is directly in the obvious and logical product roadmap path of a big company and you can block and frustrate the heck out of them by not allowing them the obvious progression in their development. (Or force them to buy you, to the delight of your investors.)

3. You end up being the first to seek and receive a patent for something that becomes very commonly used by the time the patent issues.

However, none of these scenarios is a slam-dunk money-maker. In the first scenario, you still need to go build a company to service the market. You have an IP advantage that can be used to keep others from copying you, which may give you an edge on your route to building a valuable company, but it will be up to you to enforce that advantage, and it might be very expensive.

In the second scenario, the only way you make money is to threaten that you will sue the big company if they try to move into the area covering your patent. Effectively, you are going out and trying to set up a toll booth. Any money you make off of this patent will be indirect - you are hoping they will be forced to buy or license the patent.

> In effect, patents are nothing more than a right to sue to maintain a fence around an area. It is up to the company to make being in that area valuable.

In the third scenario, you are basically a patent troll. Your business model for getting money from the patent boils down to chasing everyone in the market who adopted the patented technology and forcing them to pay license fees.

Q

So why do investors focus so much on patents?

Three reasons:

1. **Trading Card Theory**: Patents can have real defensive value as trading cards. If you build up a decent portfolio in a competitive space, and someone comes after you asserting one of their patents, it can be a life-saver to have a few of your own to counter-assert.

2. **Lottery Ticket Theory**: Occasionally patents can be exceptionally valuable, for example in the drug discovery space. If you get a patent on a critical element of a drug targeting a multi-billion dollar market, that can be worth a lot of money. Since they are a relatively affordable lottery ticket to acquire (and I do mean relatively - they are by no means cheap), it is considered standard practice to pursue them to one degree or another in certain industries.

3. **Exit Value Theory**: Even though a small start-up might not have the

bandwidth or resources to aggressively enforce a patent portfolio, a big strategic buyer might, and such a buyer might be convinced to buy a particular start up or pay a lot more for it *if the alternative is to have a potentially bothersome patent portfolio fall into the hands of a competitor*.

juice the value of an exit many years down the road.

Q

So what are the Diligence implications in all this?

You have to:

- Understand which patent theory is relevant to the company.

- Make sure the effort and expense being expended is proportional to the outcome being sought.

- Prevent a company from going to either extreme.

The company should neither be over-confident about the value of their patent portfolio, nor totally dismissive of the potential value of a few key patents, even if only held as defensive insurance or something to

Chapter 5

If You Build It, Will They Come? -Verifying Customer Demand

How often have you heard about a new product and thought "what a great idea", only to find out later that the product failed miserably? It happens all the time... and I mean ALL THE TIME! As consumers of technology, we are inundated with new products on a daily basis. Many of these products serve a useful purpose, but they don't change our lives or our productivity in a meaningful way.

So before you accept an entrepreneur's premise that her product will rule the world, step back and assess whether she's really got a game-changer. Speaking with customers and prospects is a central part of any solid due diligence process. But how you do it matters a great deal. If you ask superficial questions, you will always hear positive answers. You have to get into the mindset of a future buyer to understand how useful this new product will be.

Q

Ham, I have heard you talk about "oxygen, aspirin and jewelry." What does that mean and how do you go about the process of determining whether a product is "aspirin" or "oxygen"?

I start with the following question: Is the product a 'Nice-to-Have' or a 'Need-to-Have'? Aspirin helps reduce pain but isn't critical for survival, so it is a nice-to-have product. However, you can't live without oxygen so it is a need-to-have item. Keep in mind that this is

a continuum, and that the real difference between the two categories is just a market size question and a question about buying priorities - inevitably with any given product, the oxygen buyers are just a subset of the aspirin buyers - there are always more customers who look at it like aspirin than oxygen. For a start-up the questions are: (1) can you get to the oxygen folks early on to give the company a toehold and (2) are there ultimately enough reachable aspirin buyers to make for a big market and grow a big company?

With that in mind, my diligence process is simple. I reach out to current customers and prospects for the company's product. During my customer checks, I focus some of my initial questions on understanding the customer's key pain points and try to discern their buying priorities. I ask the following three questions:

• What problem does the product solve for you?

• On your list of the top problems in your organization, where does solving this problem fall on your priority list?

- Is your company generally an early or late adopter of new solutions?

By asking these three questions, you learn a lot. First of all, you hear in the customer's words what problems are solved by the product. Does that match what you are hearing from the entrepreneur in her pitch? If not, this is useful information you can pass back to the entrepreneur. If it does match, then you know the entrepreneur is doing a good job of listening to the customer.

> During my customer checks, I focus some of my initial questions on understanding the customer's key pain points and try to discern their buying priorities.

With the answer to the second question, you are gaining critical insight helping you gauge where the product falls on the aspirin/oxygen spectrum. If the customer tells you that the product solves one of his

top three problems, you are in Oxygen territory. Anything outside of the top 3 priorities and you are now in Aspirin territory. But don't rely on just one or two customer reference checks. This is one area where you need to dig deep during your due diligence! By talking only to one or two early adopters it is very easy to fool yourself into thinking there is more demand for a product and a larger market than there really is.

Q

What can you tell us about the buying habits of early adopters versus the buying habits of mainstream customers?

In most cases, initial customers for a tech startup will inevitably end up fitting the classic "early adopter" profile. Early adopters in the consumer space are easy to recognize.

- They are the ones willing to buy from a new company with no established track record.

- They are the ones who are happy to show off the latest new electronic gadget.

- They are the ones waiting in long lines whenever Apple releases a new iPhone.

- And, they are the ones with a closet full of last year's wonder products.

In the corporate world, early adopters tend to be either really hungry small players looking for absolutely any edge they can get to help them compete or leading technologists in large corporations. The big company technologists have a mandate from senior management to be on the lookout for new productivity enhancing products, and they have significant budgets to pay for pilots and test installations of all these new products. Since part of their job is to stay on top of new technology trends, it doesn't matter to them whether a product is Aspirin or Oxygen. And, just like your friend with the closet full of electronic toys, it's not unusual for the corporate early adopter to undertake many dead end beta evaluations - in

effect, to have dozens of forgotten products in his proverbial closet.

> It's not unusual for the corporate early adopter to undertake many dead end beta evaluations - in effect, to have dozens of forgotten products in his proverbial closet.

It's important to recognize this type of customer for the role they play in the ecosystem. They provide early feedback to the startup company on the quality and usefulness of a product. They sometimes act as references and write reviews or participate in press releases or whitepapers on products that influence "mainstream" customers. But, early adopters represent a VERY small percentage of the overall market, and their desires and needs are different than the majority. Though startup founders make this mistake every day, interest from early adopters should NEVER be confused with market traction or true customer validation. Although early adopters are important, when doing diligence we must speak with the larger mainstream customer base to gauge the true customer need. A startup company will not grow beyond a few million dollars in revenue if it can't Cross the Chasm and sell to mainstream customers. And mainstream customers are always going to have more oxygen products than aspirin products at the top of their buying priority list. To be successful, you are either going to have to come up with a product that is oxygen to a lot of customers, or be really good at marketing aspirin.

Q

How do you pull together a list of customers / prospects to call?

I start with the list of key customers and prospects that are provided by the company. This list is usually relatively short -- say 2 to 4 contacts. It represents the contacts that the company expects will provide glowing reports. And, most likely, it will be a bunch of early adopters who represent a small slice of the overall market.

Next, I work with our due diligence team to draw up a list of prospects we believe might be interested in the product. These prospects should come from the more mainstream segment of the target market. At Launchpad, we invest in businesses where we have expertise. Part of that expertise includes having influential contacts at key target customers. If you don't have those types of contacts when you are performing your diligence, you are exposing yourself to market risk. One clever way to find mainstream customers to call is to ask the company-provided contacts who their competitors are.

If possible, try to connect the company to potential sales opportunities with these prospective customers. The feedback you will receive from these sales calls should prove instructive in assessing the "Need to Have" level of the company's product. In many cases it is equally important to talk with the company's partners or prospective partners for their perspective on the "need to have" requirement.

Remember that these partners are some of the most likely acquirers of the company.

> Although early adopters are important, when doing diligence we must speak with the larger mainstream customer base to gauge the true customer need. A startup company will not grow beyond a few million dollars in revenue if it can't Cross the Chasm and sell to mainstream customers.

Q

Is it difficult to find customers and prospects to speak to?

In general, it's not hard to find people who are willing to give you feedback on a new product or service. If the company doesn't even have a prototype to demonstrate, their feedback is based on their perception of what they believe the product will do for them. Without something to actually interact with, their input to you will be of limited value.

Let's look at a couple of examples. What if the company is building a new medical device that simplifies a complex surgical procedure. With just a set of CAD drawings, a surgeon can only imagine whether the device will help, and justifiably, she will be reluctant to give a positive recommendation, or if she does, it will be based on her conception of what the product *might* be able to do for her.

Now, imagine a new video game. It's based on the latest in Virtual Reality technology. But, all the company can show you is some artist renderings of what the virtual world will look like. How are you going to find out if their target market of males between 16 and 24 will make this new game a big hit?

In both these examples, the stage of the company's product limits the value of customer due diligence. You will have to rely on your own expertise and maybe a few of your most trusted industry contacts.

Q

How do you handle sensitivity around speaking to customers and not spooking them away from this early startup?

It's not unusual for a CEO to be hyper-sensitive when investors call their customers. They worry that customers will freak out because the investor might raise red flags about the long term viability of the company. Personally, I believe that CEOs are justified in thinking this way. If investors aren't sensitive to this situation, they can cause the company harm. So how do you go about asking questions in a way that

puts everyone at ease and gets you the answers you need for your diligence report?

> It's not unusual for a CEO to be hyper-sensitive when investors call their customers. They worry that customers will freak out because the investor might raise red flags about the long term viability of the company.

First of all, I set the stage by describing why I am calling. I tell the customer that I am a prospective investor and looking to help the company reach the next level of success. I frame my introduction in a way that should ease their concerns. Next, I start with questions about the customer's business and what problems they are solving with this new product. In most cases, the customer is very willing to open up about their issues and challenges. And remember, the answers to these questions are critical in helping you understand buying priorities - whether the product is Aspirin or Oxygen.

Depending on how open the customer's initial responses are, I might dig deep and ask tougher questions, or I might limit our conversation to the basics related to Aspirin vs. Oxygen. And, I always end the call by saying something positive about the start-up company and thanking the buyer representative for their time and help with my research. By keeping a positive tone throughout the call, we can usually limit any concerns that the customer might have about the startup company.

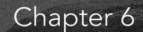

Chapter 6

Room To Run - Startup Uniqueness & Competition

How many times have you heard an entrepreneur say they have no competition? After hearing thousands of investor pitches over the years, my rough estimate is that I hear it about 25% of the time. When I hear a CEO blurt this out, I chuckle to myself and think, well, maybe there isn't a need for their product. Or, maybe the CEO is just clueless about their target market.

Competition for new "Need to Have" products always exists. Researching the competition and providing reasonably detailed discussions about the competition will be a joint effort between the company and the due diligence team. Moreover, even the best of startup teams will learn valuable information as they review the competition and better understand their own uniqueness in their target market.

Q

Christopher, how do you kick off a competitive review?

In most cases, you can start by asking the company to provide a detailed list of competitors. Don't accept the company's list without checking the ecosystem they live in to find competitors they might have left out. And, once you've built up this additional list, make sure the company provides you with their key differentiators.

It is also important to use a "mindshare" or "walletshare" lens

when thinking about competition. The four fiercest competitors most products face are;

1. **Ignorance** about your product (they might like it, but they have just not been educated yet)

2. **Alternates**/substitutes from other categories (i.e. not movie A vs movie B, but dinner out instead of a movie)

3. **Fear of change** (which is how everyone except the early adopters thinks)

4. The **inertia** of "good enough" (which requires a major catalyst to overcome)

The existence of these four tough competitors drives a harsh reality: just because the new product is better than the competing products, doesn't mean it will sell. As noted in Chapter 4, it often needs to be 10X better.

> Don't accept the company's list without checking the ecosystem they live in to find competitors they might have left out.

Q

During your customer reference checks, the feedback indicated that the entrepreneur is selling a real "Need to Have" product. How do you determine if the product is differentiated and defensible?

First of all, to determine if the product is differentiated, we do a competitive analysis that combines our own research along with market outreach to customers and prospects. During our reference calls, we ask the following questions:

- How are you solving your problem today?

- Have you used similar products before?

- Did you look at any competitive products?

- Are you considering any alternative ways of solving the problem?

It's important during this stage of due diligence that you have one or two market experts helping with your research. You don't want to be blindsided by a competitor that was already very well-established in the market.

The key when looking for differentiation is to look for distinctions that matter to the customer. Founders are in love with their product. They know every detail. They are really close to the nitty gritty - usually too close. When asked about differentiation, founders won't hesitate to cite differences which are extremely nuanced. Even if they can even be detected by the typical hurried customer, they often will not be a major value driver from the customer's perspective. The investor's job is to figure out the differentiators that matter to the customer and make sure they are present in the product.

Q

OK, so how do you determine if the product is defensible?

To determine if the product is defensible, we need to look at three basic questions:

- Can the hard won customers be retained?

- Will pricing power hold up over time?

- Are the margins in the business likely to be squeezed by competitive or environmental factors?

Retaining customers is all about delivering a strong value-proposition relative to your price and relative to the other things on the market. You need to get to a bottom line: does the company have a compelling offering?

Defending pricing and margins usually takes one of two forms: either keeping competitors out through some sort of blocking rights like intellectual property (e.g. public forms such as patents, trademarks, copyright or private forms such as

trade secrets or proprietary know how), or finding ways to keep customers in.

> The key when looking for differentiation is to look for distinctions that matter to the customer... The investor's job is to figure out the differentiators that matter to the customer and make sure they are present in the product.

Keeping customers in requires some form of the classic economic concept of high-switching costs. In the case of Facebook, the high switching costs would be all the friends, updates, photos and data you have collected on the system and cannot figure out how to move elsewhere. On a personal computer platform it might be all the software you have invested in which is only compatible with that platform. In cameras, it might be getting someone to invest in a lot of Nikon lenses over time so they will never switch camera brands. In case it is not obvious, businesses with high switching costs are not that easy to build, especially in today's internet-centric world where competitors' products are just a quick Google search away. It is also worth noting in the context of forecasting, more often than not, efforts to bake in switching costs just come across as product limitations which irritate consumers and slow adoption. Consumers are pretty savvy at avoiding lock-in and format wars when they can. As much as it hurts to admit it, sometimes the best lock-ins are an accident, or at least very subtle and sneaky in the beginning.

One closing thought here: "first mover advantage" is not a type of defensibility. Entrepreneurs cite it all the time, but as we have discussed in the past, getting an actual advantage from being a first mover is really rare and really hard.

> Speaking with the customer references about the market and the competitors and the value proposition can be incredibly enlightening. It is amazing what people will open up and tell you if you just take the time to ask in a nice way.

Q

How do you determine the level of competitive intensity and noise in a market?

Silly as it sounds, in today's world, searching the web is a good place to start. The entrepreneur will generally include a slide with competitors and a slide with potential acquirers, so you always have a place to start. Checking out those companies' websites to get a sense of the level of marketing sophistication and effort will give you a good sense of what the start-up is up against. These websites will also give you a sense of key features being touted and sometimes even competitive pricing information.

In more mature industries there may be third party analyst reports such as the classic industry analyst magic quadrant, studies, forecasts and journalism. These can be excellent sources of information to help you understand who the players are, what the customer dynamics are, and what the main selling points seem to be.

And finally, speaking with the customer references about the market and the competitors and the value proposition can be incredibly enlightening. It is amazing what people will open up and tell you if you just take the time to ask in a nice way.

Q

So let's assume that the company has a solid lead in the market. How do you factor in issues such as defensibility of market share and price/margins?

It is very important to look at company growth forecasts in the context of the overall growth of the market. It is not uncommon for companies to give you projections that have them owning ridiculous amounts of market share. Every market is different, and some newer markets will grow much faster than more mature markets, so you need to look at the plan and understand what the revenue forecasts imply. Put another way, it is great that a company says they are doubling every year, but if their market share would actually be shrinking over the same period, that has some pretty major implications.

Likewise, if that doubling growth rate implies that they are going to be going from 20% to 60% to 80% market share, you might want to dig a little deeper into the projections. It pays to keep in mind that the faster your company projects it can grow, the more likely that is going to be an attractive market into which new forms of competition will flow. And it won't always be companies just like yours - it will often be much deeper pocketed companies who suddenly wake up to the strategic importance of the market and are not only able, but happy to subsidize their solution to gain share quickly. In short, market conditions are like the weather - it can change very quickly.

Q

Where do substitutes and/or adjacent solutions fit into your competitive review?

As noted above, it is very important to understand that very meaningful competition can come not only from similar products but also ***doing it an entirely different way***, or even ***not doing it at all***. Founders who are very close to the product, virtually steeped in nuances that may or may not ultimately matter to customers, can have a very skewed, but also very contagious perspective. And it

is not helped by the fact that customer conversations at this stage are exclusively with early adopters.

It is very important to understand that very meaningful competition can come not only from similar products but also *doing it an entirely different way*, or even *not doing it at all*.

You need to step back and find out what people are doing now, what other alternatives they have to the company's proposed solution and what benefits (as opposed to features or nuances) they bring to the party. Competitors will be going out of their way to provide alternatives to the product, history and inertia will provide substitutes for the product, and established players will extend their product suites to provide weak but trusted counterfeits of the product. Your job is to figure out how much those

55

alternative paths matter; does the company have something that provides really compelling value?

Q

Do you spend much time thinking about prospective competitors or new technologies that might disrupt the market?

Yes, depending on the industry, that can be time well spent. For example, Cisco paid a half a billion dollars for a stand-alone video camera company (Flip Video) at a time when cell phones already had crude cameras. It would be one thing if phones didn't yet have cameras, but many would argue the rapid demise of Flip was totally foreseeable had Cisco only taking the trouble to think about it. Taking a moment to look at the technology in the market, not as a lake of standing water but as a river of moving water (or if you want a more apt analogy, as a movie not a snapshot), can allow you to see not where things are, but where things are going.

In other words, you should be thinking not about where the company is competing, but where it is going to be competing. For example, in today's world, there are dozens of businesses that were recently eaten by the smartphone with its sensors, always-on connectivity and powerfully flexible UI. Just look at Garmin's several hundred million dollar per year stand-alone GPS business - poof; gone overnight. Same thing with MP3 players and iPods - poof. In fact, virtually anybody who launched an overlapping product in the last 10 years and who underestimated the speed at which smartphones were going to improve, quickly got crushed. There is a great story from a watershed moment when the CEO of RIM/Blackberry first heard about the iPhone. Up to that time, the entire industry had been trying to scale up and do more with weak low power mobile chips and mobile operating systems (OS). When the CEO heard what the iPhone could do, he realized with a chilling shudder that Apple had gone in a completely opposite direction - they had shrunk a desktop computer and OS. And it was game over for all the heritage product lines virtually overnight.

The lesson here is to try to escape the present and project some of the more obvious new behaviors and technologies farther out into the future. Perhaps the most powerful example of this thinking is Google's tendency to look at problems by asking "what would you do to solve this if bandwidth and computing power were infinite and free? They soon will be, so go do it now."

Footnote: This answer would not be complete if it did not point out that it is possible to get badly burned by *overestimating* the rate of change too. Many investors have been wrong in assuming things will be adopted more quickly than they are. So how does an investor reconcile that contradiction? By recognizing that different assumptions are at play. Technology almost always moves quickly, but changes in customer behavior almost never do (at least until they reach a critical tipping point). Nobody ever got rich overestimating the customer's speed of adoption nor underestimating the pace of technological change.

Q

How does a competitive review inform your view on the strength of the CEO?

Two very important ways:

First, it provides an insight into their knowledge of the market - do they know who the competitors are, are they keeping tabs, have they studied customer needs closely. If a CEO cannot add value and perspective to the competitive assessment, or doesn't seem interested, that is a major red flag.

Second, it gives you a gauge of their ability to be visionary and deal with abstractions and hypotheticals. Some people are plodders - content to optimize for the here and now. Great CEOs are not satisfied with the status quo - they are looking way ahead and determined to drive things forward.

Chapter 7

What the Market Will Bear - Evaluating Go to Market Strategies

We are all familiar with how technology made dramatic changes in our lives over the past few years. Computers, the Internet, mobile phones, etc. all conspired to make our lives more efficient and more chaotic! And, these disruptive changes touched all aspects of how companies run their operations. It's not surprising that Sales and Marketing professionals have seen some of the biggest changes in how they operate their day-to-day tasks.

Marketing used to be all about PR and Advertising. Now, if you don't understand Content Marketing and how to apply Data Analytics to dig into your customer's behavior you won't be effective. With Sales, you need to understand that your customer knows a lot about your product even before you talk to them. Customers are able to research both you and your competition without engaging a salesperson.

As an investor in early stage companies, you must be aware of the new world order in Sales and Marketing before you are able to understand whether a company is well positioned to achieve success in their Go-to-Market Strategy. That said, many of the old rules about how to successfully go to market are still in place. Sales and marketing is still work and it still costs money. It is just different kinds of work and spend. So what are we looking for in an early stage company that may or may not have any customers?

Q

Ham, when a CEO is presenting the company's Go-to-Market strategy, what are some of the key points you are listening for?

The CEO has to be specific about how the company is going to crack their market. Selling is really hard, especially to certain types of customers. S/he will need to convince investors that the company has a very detailed plan or business model innovation that is going to allow the company to acquire their intended customers affordably (relative to their life-time value).

Key questions that an investor must ask include:

- Is the company selling with a direct sales force, over the web, through partners, through distributors?

- Where are the customers and how will they locate them, talk to them, and bring them on board cost-effectively?

- What is the customer acquisition cost (CAC) going to be relative to the lifetime value (LTV) of the customer? (Hint: LTV better be higher than CAC, or they're in trouble.)

There are many different Go-to-Market strategies and they vary from industry to industry. Since we can't dig into all the possible strategies, let me give one example from an industry that I know well, the Software-as-a-Service (SaaS) market.

> As an investor in early stage companies, you must be aware of the new world order in Sales and Marketing before you are able to understand whether a company is well-positioned to achieve success in their Go-to-Market Strategy.

If you are going to invest in a SaaS company, the CEO will need to describe which of the following approaches the company will use to acquire customers. In the list that follows, I name the approach and then put a dollar range that represents how much you should expect it will cost to acquire one customer (i.e. CAC).

- Freemium ($0 - $50)
- No Touch Self-Service ($50 - $250)
- Light Touch Inside Sales ($250 - $2,000)
- High Touch Inside Sales ($2,000 - $10,000)
- Field Sales ($10,000+)

In the early days of a startup company, you want sales people who are willing to do the grunt work of opening a new market and closing sales. You don't want a CEO who is looking to build a large sales organization before the company figures out a scalable Go-to-Market strategy.

Once you know how the company is going to sell product, there are a handful of metrics that you must understand to get a sense for whether the company has a viable, scalable Go-to-Market plan. The metrics are as follows:

- **Customer Acquisition Cost** (CAC) - This cost will vary depending on how the company sells its product (see bullet list above - but you will need to verify that their costs align with this list)

- **Months to Recover CAC** - In an ideal world, the company will be able to recover CAC in under twelve months. Anything greater than two years is a red flag.

- **Customer Churn Rate** - Companies with a low churn rate (e.g. under 1% customer loss per month) can grow faster without having to raise as much capital

- **Life-Time Value** (LTV) of a Customer - If you can find a company with LTV more than three times CAC, then you've found a great investment opportunity

For early stage SaaS companies that are just starting to ship product, it will be difficult to get accurate numbers for each of these metrics. That said, the company's financial plan should reflect the reality of these metrics. Make sure their assumptions in the financial plan are reasonable based on their Go-to-Market strategy.

Q

With an early stage company, what are you expecting to see when it comes to the Sales & Marketing team?

As an early stage investor, I am used to investing in companies where the team is small. In many cases the CEO is the chief salesperson and the company might not have any full time marketing people. But that lack of a formal sales organization shouldn't scare you away from investing. In fact, I am sometimes more worried when a company has a high powered VP of Sales who comes from a big company background and is accustomed to having a staff and doing things according to conventional wisdom.

In the early days of a startup company, you want sales people who are willing to do the grunt work of opening a new market and closing sales. You don't want a CEO who is looking to build a large sales organization before the company figures out a scalable Go-to-Market strategy. That's the fastest way to burn through your investment without producing results - nail it before you scale it!

> In the early days of a startup company, you want sales people who are willing to do the grunt work of opening a new market and closing sales. You don't want a CEO who is looking to build a large sales organization before the company figures out a scalable Go-to-Market strategy.

Often, some of the dollars we are investing will be used to hire a few sales and/or marketing people. In an ideal situation, the initial sales talent are self-directed individuals who don't need much training to sell to the target customer. And with marketing, the early hires are individuals with experience building compelling content and filling the top of the sales funnel with qualified leads.

Q

As we mention in the introduction, Marketing changed dramatically over the past several years. Can you be more specific as to what you look for in the marketing plan for a startup?

Isn't going viral how everybody grows these days?? Just kidding... I cringe when an entrepreneur proclaims the company will grow just by word-of-mouth. I know it can happen on the rare occasion, but I wouldn't want to bet the farm on it!

With early stage companies, it can take a while before you figure out what marketing programs will work best for the business. And, it's not unusual for a plan that's successful in the early days of the company to lose momentum as the company matures and the customer base evolves from early adopter, to early majority to mainstream.

So at the point in time when we are doing our diligence, I am not looking for a set of marketing programs with a detailed 12 month marketing calendar. Instead, I expect to see answers to the following questions:

- **Market Segmentation**: Who is the target customer(s)?

- **Market Opportunity**: How many customers are out there? How much are they willing to spend?

- **Marketing Channels**: Where will you find them? How will you reach them?

Chapter 8

Big Enough To Be Interesting - Market Size and Opportunity

Market Opportunity is an important metric for estimating the long-term potential for an early stage company. Typically, we invest in companies that are going after market sizes of at least $100M. At that size, a market is large enough to support a $25M+ company. Many early stage companies are opening up new markets, so determining overall market size is not easy. We recommend attacking this problem from several angles.

It is important when looking at market opportunity to do your best to gauge how much customers are willing to pay for the product, since this will be a key driver of top line revenues. Don't rely solely on information from the company. Rather, you and your team should try to develop your own assessment of the market opportunity. Talking to potential partners of the company who are already in the market can provide useful information. This is information you will use to assess whether this is a lifestyle company or one that has a likely exit.

As an active angel investor, Christopher looks at hundreds of companies every year. Some are tackling big problems in huge markets. Others are going after undiscovered challenges in specialized or emerging markets. At first blush, most investors would choose the former investment opportunity over the latter. But you will have to dig a bit deeper to understand whether you've made the right choice. So let's see what Christopher's years of experience have done for his market sleuthing skills.

Q

Christopher, what characteristics do you think make for an interesting, investable market opportunity for startup companies?

In a perfect world, I am looking for a market that is worth going after and offers an opportunity to build non-linear growth - very steep growth curves. By "worth going after" I basically mean big enough and durable enough over the long term (i.e. product needs which are not just a fad). By "opportunity to ... grow," I am talking about market conditions which are going to allow companies to accrete value to the entity much faster than they spend the entity's resources (cash/equity). In an established market, that means growing faster than the overall market growth and thereby taking market share. In a new market, that means educating and acquiring customers for much less than the lifetime value of those customers.

Brand new markets are very tough to estimate in size. Your best estimate can be wildly off on both the downside or the upside. Startups routinely overestimate their markets. Even the CEO of IBM once said the worldwide market opportunity for computers was only 5 machines! In evaluating the new market opportunity, you look for genuine pull from customers and you watch out for false demand from unsustainable marketing practices.

In a perfect world, I am looking for a market that is worth going after and offers an opportunity to build non-linear growth - very steep growth curves.

Failed startup HomeJoy is a great example of the kind of trouble you can get into with delusional thinking. They raised tens of millions of dollars in venture capital and were using it to offer their $100 cleaning services through bargain sites, like Groupon, for $19. Predictably, none of those bargain-hunting customers came back as repeat customers (and who knows if they had really dirty houses that hadn't been cleaned in a while.) Spending $100 to acquire a crappy $19 customer who does not stick around is roughly equivalent to picking up a spade and digging your own grave.

With established markets you are looking for places where the market and the solutions on offer are kind of "stuck" in one way or another. These are the opportunities you can pounce on. For example, the market might be:

- Really fragmented with a ton of small players, and waiting for a break-out leader.

- Old and calcified and totally ripe for disruption by a new entrant with a new edge.

- Really fast changing where customers are starting to flock and can be picked off before they settle on a competitor.

One favorite situation of mine is an industry where a technical innovation or solution is sorely needed. Typically, no one particular industry participant is going to build the solution. If they did, they would not recoup the expenses because they would build it to suit their needs only and they wouldn't want to give it to their competitors, even if they could. Third parties can come into a market like this with a new and better way of doing it, and solve critical problems for everybody in the industry as a neutral third party. Salesforce.com is but one example of that.

One final observation is that whatever the market, the investor syndicate must include active investors with deep experience in some aspect of the market. Maybe they have worked with these same customers in another context, or they have deep expertise with the technology, or they have built a very similar business in an adjacent space. Ideally you would have all three in the group.

> Whatever the market, the investor syndicate must include active investors with deep experience in some aspect of the market.

Q

Is there a minimum size to a potential market below which you won't invest? If so, why won't you invest?

Well, it is hard for early stage equity investors to make the numbers work with a market less than $100M in total size. It is basic arithmetic. Here is why: early stage investors need to be able to credibly model a 10X return at the outset of every investment, since so many companies fail. If, ...

- They are only going to own part of the company, and

- The company is going to have way less than 100% market share, and

- The company is likely to be acquired for a revenue or EBITDA multiple of less than 10X...

Then the arithmetic won't work for much less than a $100M market.

Let's look at a couple examples. Let's say a company ends up with 5% of a billion dollar market, and the early investors put in a total of $4M in early rounds and end up holding about 12% of the company after dilution from later rounds. And let's give the company a good but reasonable revenue multiple from a buyer of, say, 7X. In that scenario, the company is worth 7 times $50M revenue (5% of a $1B market) or a total exit valuation of $350M. In that scenario, the early stage investors end up with $42M for their 12% of the $350M, which is a solid 10X return.

If you run that same model with a much smaller market and no adjustments, it is a terrible result: for example let's say a company ends up with 5% of a $100M dollar market, and the early investors put in a total of $4M in early rounds and ended up holding about 12% of the company after dilution from later

rounds. And let's give the company the same revenue multiple from a buyer of 7X. In that scenario, the company is worth 7 times $5M in revenue or a total valuation of $35M on the company. In that scenario, the early stage investors end up with $4.2M for their 12%, which is a break-even 1X return.

What is really interesting is that if you re-run the scenario with some reasonable adjustments to reflect a lighter capitalization due to a smaller market, and a higher attainable market share percentage, you still don't get a great result. Even if you stipulate that the investors end up owning two times as much of the market share and you stipulate that they raise significantly less money, you are still looking at half of the desired model return.

For the sake of completeness, here's how those smaller company, smaller market numbers look. The company ends up with 10% of a $100M market (twice the market share in percentage terms of the previous example), and the early investors ended up putting in $3M ($1M less in early equity), and they end up owning 20% of the company (twice as much of the company because they were diluted less since the company raised less money). The company gets acquired for the same 7X revenue (which is probably overly generous for a market this size, if you could even find a strategic buyer for a $10M run-rate company). So they are bought for 7 times $10M or $70M, and the investors get $14M of that for their 20%. Given that they put $3M in, that is a 4.6X return.

> At the end of the day, your true market consists exclusively of those people for whom your solution is a top buying priority, plus any additional customers you can profitably convince to make it a top buying priority.

One can play with the numbers and assumptions a bit…

- Given the high risk of outright failure in this type of early stage investing

- The near total lack of liquidity prior to exit

- The amount of time it would take a startup to get 10% of a $100M market

- The time it would take to find a buyer willing to pay 7X for the company

A 1.0X - 4.6X range of best-case return is much less attractive than going after a bigger market. So the $100M market probably represents the absolute floor in market size, absent of special circumstances.

Q

One of my pet peeves with investor presentations occurs when an entrepreneur states they are going after the $400B XYZ market, when in reality they are going after a small segment of this huge market. How do you go about determining the real size of the addressable market for a startup?

It all comes back to customer buying priorities. You can talk all you want about how big your potential addressable market is, but at the end of the day, your true market consists exclusively of those people for whom your solution is a top buying priority, plus any additional customers you can profitably convince to make it a top buying priority. As I said in my Q&A on the importance of due diligence, it is very easy and very tempting to confuse early adopter excitement with true market pull. It has been said that "anybody can get the first 10% of a market," and Geoffrey Moore's Crossing the Chasm stands for that proposition.

The key to growing a company is finding a big enough market of willing buyers who can be accessed in an affordable way (relative to their lifetime value). The product may be good, and there may be lots of people who might buy it, but unfortunately a company's true market is limited to those customers for whom that purchase addresses a top pain point and a top buying priority. See Chapter 5 on Oxygen, Aspirin & Jewelry. Often a marginal improvement on a marginal cost is not enough to drive buying behavior in all but the earliest of adopters. So the key is to recognize when you are looking at what is sometimes called false traction and do some further digging. There is no substitute for talking to real customers and prospects before making an investment in these situations.

Q

A colleague of mine at one of my prior startup companies had a favorite expression. "More companies die of overeating than starvation." What do you think he meant by this?

This can mean one of two things, and sometimes both! The first form of startup gluttony is losing focus, and the second is pouring resources into unproven hunches before there is enough basis for doing so. For start-ups, focus and prioritization are everything, and it is critical to spend resources wisely and in a targeted way. Companies overeat by taking too much on, losing focus on what is important, and hiring and taking on the costs of trying to scale before there is a solid basis for doing so. From a diligence perspective the key is to review and agree on the strategic plan, the use of proceeds, and the milestones to be achieved before raising the next round and ramping up the spend.

Q

One of the popular buzz phrases for VCs these days, is "Product / Market Fit". What do they mean by this and what should you look for during due diligence?

Product / Market Fit is a very simple concept which refers to the moment when you have a product that meets the needs of a large market segment. It is often used in conjunction with the term "minimum viable product" because, during your search for fit, you are generally trying to build as little unwanted product as possible.

From a diligence perspective, determining product / market fit is tricky because there are very few data points.

So you create what you think will be the minimum viable product for a target market and test and iterate until you suddenly see pull. Your pipeline of leads begins to grow, your cost of sales begins to drop, your sales cycle begins to shorten and your average revenue per customer starts to grow. That is when you know you have product / market fit and you can begin pouring on the gas in search of accelerated growth.

From a diligence perspective, determining product / market fit is tricky because there are very few data points. So it's as if you are trying to read tea leaves. It can take months of experimentation to find product / market fit, and so it is often necessary to raise money before the company has found it. There is a tendency to want to believe, at face value, the positive story the founders have spun based on a couple good months in a row. But you need to dig deeper to really understand what you are looking at. You may still invest prior to product / market fit, but you need to recognize what you are doing, size the round modestly, and establish a cost-effective path to find it.

Chapter 9

Does It Compute?
Financials and Funding
Strategy

Raise your hand if you've ever been in this situation: You meet
with an entrepreneur, and his pitch is awesome! The team is
great, the product is great... everything is great. Except, the
team is seriously deficient when it comes to understanding
finances.

You were ready to write a check. But you are a thoughtful investor who doesn't make quick decisions just based on gut feeling. So you put your checkbook away and commit to some serious financial due diligence. It's time to roll up your sleeves, pull out the green eyeshade and dig into the financial plan and funding strategy for this awesome new company.

Those of you who aren't numbers people are probably tempted to skip this article. You should read on, because you really need to know this stuff or, I promise, it will come back to bite you! That said, if you truly aren't into understanding a company's finances, make sure you have someone on the due diligence team who is.

Even though I spent some time as the CFO of a public enterprise software company, it is Ham who is the financial genius at Launchpad and Seraf. He does all our financial planning and is on the audit committee for several company boards. So he really digs this financial stuff. Why, I don't know.

Q

Ham, we have a lot of ground to cover, so let's jump right in. What's the first thing you look for in a company's financial plan?

Behind every solid financial plan, I expect to find a rationally thought out and verifiable set of key assumptions. These assumptions should be reasonable and not in conflict with core elements of the business plan and the market being served. For example, the unit price for the company's product should be within reason.

> Behind every solid financial plan, I expect to find a rationally thought out and verifiable set of key assumptions.

So if the company projects a $1000 unit sale price for their product and the competition sells their similar product for under $10, you will need to ask some questions as to why there is such a significant price differential.

Different industries have very different key assumptions that drive the financial plan. That said, there are a core set of assumptions that all plans should be based upon. Some of the key assumptions made in the preparation of financial projections should include:

- Is the company's **long term funding plan** connected to specific milestones such as first prototype, Beta test completion, FDA approval, pilot production, First Customer Ship (FCS), etc.?

- When will the company **reach cash flow breakeven/positive** and how much funding will be required to reach this point?

- Have **unit sales volumes** been tied to rational sales cycles and seasonality?

- Are **market penetration rates** consistent with the market sizing and competitive conditions shown in the Business Plan?

- Do **Average Sales Prices** (ASPs) link to market comparables and anticipate future competitive pricing pressures?

- Is **gross margin** as a percentage of revenue what you would expect to generate for this product when stacked up to market comparables?

- Have **projected staff salaries** been derived from current market/ labor conditions?

Q

Most entrepreneurs include a section in their presentation on amount of financing they are raising and the use of proceeds. What do you look for here?

Near the end of the CEO's pitch to investors, they always ask for money. And, in most cases, they give a very high level overview of where the money will be spent. A typical presentation might break the spending down as follows: (40% for engineering, 30% for sales and marketing, and 30% for operations).

That's a start, but you need to know more. After you've examined the key assumptions in the financial plan, the next step is to dig into the use of proceeds. First and foremost, you should understand what milestones will be achieved with the proceeds from the financing. Let's look at two examples:

1. A medical device company is raising $500K. With this financing, the company expects to build a prototype of their product and start initial animal testing.

2. A software company is raising $1.5M. Their product is built and they already have their first customers. With this financing, the company expects to grow to $200K in Monthly Recurring Revenue (MRR) and to approach Cash Flow Breakeven (CFBE).

I like to see a monthly financial plan that provides realistic expenses that result in meeting key milestones. That tells me that the CEO (and her team) understand what it takes to move the company to the next stage. But, we're not done yet. You need to take it one step further. You need to understand how significant

those milestones are. Here are a couple of the questions you should ask:

- Will this increase the value of the company and the investment I am going to make?

- Will new investors be interested in continuing to finance the company, and help it reach its ultimate goal of a successful acquisition or IPO?

If you can't answer these questions in the affirmative, you have some more work to do. Maybe you need to convince the CEO to lower the valuation on the company. Or, maybe you need to help the CEO raise even more capital so the company can achieve an even greater set of milestones.

I like to see a monthly financial plan that provides realistic expenses that result in meeting key milestones.

Q

As an investor and a board member, understanding a company's financing strategy is critical. Before you make an investment in a company, what do you need to know about a company's funding plan?

As an early stage investor, my concerns are different than later stage investors. Once I am comfortable with the Key Assumptions and Milestones, I move on to explore two additional areas.

1. In the near term, how much runway does the company have before it runs out of cash?

2. In the long term, how much capital will the company need before an exit?

To answer the first question, I look at a detailed monthly P&L statement along with the cash flow statement. I want to know as accurately as possible how many months the company can operate before cash runs out. And, I want to make sure that period is long enough to allow the company to achieve the key milestones we agreed upon earlier. If it's not enough, then I will work with the company to raise more capital than they originally set out to raise.

For the second question, I am trying to figure out how much financial risk I am taking by making this investment. If the company only needs to raise a small amount of money before an exit, I can reduce financing risk to a minimum level. On the other hand, if the company will need to raise $20M+, I am taking on significant financing risk with my investment. I will need to plan accordingly by reserving a larger amount of my investment capital for future rounds of financing. And, finally, I may need to make many introductions to bigger venture investors to ensure that the company can raise what it needs to succeed.

Q

We've discussed many of the high level issues relating to a company's finances. Let's dig in a bit deeper. What are some of the critical secondary issues that investors should understand?

When you invest in a very early stage company, there aren't that many financial issues that come back to bite you. Sometimes, I do invest in companies that have a bit of history and have been in business for more than a year or two. If that's the case, then I tend to dig a bit further. It's not unusual for a startup company to defer payments with a number of their vendors, including lawyers and suppliers. So as part of our diligence, we will ask to see their balance sheet and make sure that both AP and AR are well documented. In most cases, these items will be covered by our attorneys in the closing documents' disclosure schedule. And, don't forget to make sure that the founders aren't expecting any back pay or repayment of credit card debt, unless you've fully bought into these payments!

Q

What if they have a great business opportunity but need serious help on pulling together their financial plan, what do you do?

That's a pretty easy question... I point them in the direction of a great CFO! We are fortunate in the Boston area to have access to many successful CFOs who are willing to work part time for startup companies. In the early days, startups might need a CFO for a day or two a month. During fundraising periods, that need might increase a bit. As a CEO, you are crazy not to make use of this valuable resource. A CEO might not value this skillset as highly as they do a great engineer or marketer, but never underestimate the value of a well thought out financial plan.

Chapter 10

Penalty Box - Legal Issues For Startups

It might be hard to believe, but it's not very difficult for an early stage company to run into all sorts of legal issues before they even start to ship product. The good news is that most legal issues at this stage are confined to just a few areas. With just a little research, you can ascertain whether the company has any legal cleanup needed before you are ready to sign the check and close the deal.

For most early stage companies there are four main areas where you want to concentrate your legal due diligence:

1. Intellectual Property,

2. Corporate Capitalization Structure,

3. Third Party Contracts, and

4. Employee Agreements.

Christopher has a long background in corporate law and he's seen almost every type of legal issue through the years. Entrepreneurs are crazy busy trying to get their company off the ground. Occasionally, they are known to cut corners that they wouldn't have if they had good legal advice along the way.

Q

Christopher, what are the most important issues to be aware of when you are looking at a company's Intellectual Property (IP)?

We verify clear ownership or licenses of necessary IP assets. For most early stage investments we make, verifying IP ownership is critical. In particular, we seek to ensure that the company has secured appropriate assignment of invention and non-disclosure agreements with all past and present individuals who worked on the intellectual property, whether as founders, employees, consultants or otherwise.

We seek to ensure that the company has secured appropriate assignment of invention and non-disclosure agreements with all past and present individuals who worked on the intellectual property, whether as founders, employees, consultants or otherwise.

It is also important to confirm that – to the extent the company is utilizing IP from a third party (such as an academic institution) – a company has sufficient rights for a sufficient duration of time (hopefully perpetual) to execute the business plan. You will also want to understand the economics of any licenses as well. And finally, depending on the situation, you may need to do some work to make sure the company has freedom to operate relative to patents belonging to third parties.

stock to non-founders is important both from a historical standpoint as well as from a pro forma perspective. A cap table can provide a strong "fossil record" as to the prior financing history, potential issues with legacy founders, and the current incentive structure for existing employees and founders. Looking behind the cap table can also reveal those parties that may have other claims relative to the company's stock (such as informal/contractual anti-dilution rights) that can be disruptive to a financing.

Q

We tend to be very early investors in a company. What problems could we run into with the company's capitalization structure?

We fully document and understand the capitalization structure and history of the company. Understanding each component of the cap structure, including prior financings, the vesting around existing employee equity, and some of the history behind the issuance of

Q

Many of the companies we invest in don't have any outside contracts at the time we invest, but some do. What are some of the pitfalls that startups stumble into with their early third-party contracts?

We are aware of and review any exclusive or restrictive contracts. Early stage companies sometimes do desperate/foolish things to secure a first contract or garner early bootstrap revenue. These contracts can contain provisions that:

- Grant third-parties exclusive rights with respect to technology,

- Offer very aggressive service level guarantees, warranties or indemnities,

- Divest from the company rights around a particular field of use,

- Limit the territory in which a company can compete, among other things.

Any contracts that limit a company from realizing its business plan or that sacrifice long term potential for short term viability need to be considered when evaluating the overall investment opportunity.

Q

One of the biggest assets that startup companies tend to have are their employees. What issues do we need to research when it comes to employees?

Beyond basic HR and personnel compliance, we ask about any ongoing employment issues, and verify key employee agreements and at least barebones policies and procedures are in place. In addition to confirming that the company has adequately protected its IP rights vis-a-vis employees and consultants, we need to understand a company's obligations to its employees, from promises of deferred salary and bonus to severance agreements to purported grants of equity.

> A cap table can provide a strong "fossil record" as to the prior financing history, potential issues with legacy founders, and the current incentive structure for existing employees and founders.

Often, in courting prospective employees, a naïve company will make informal promises to individuals that can form the basis for real lawsuits in the future. Wrapping our head around the past and existing employee base will

help smoke out potential, costly
issues that tend to rear their ugly
head when the company closes a
financing.

Chapter 11

Will Anyone Care?
Building an Exit Strategy

Early stage investors might not view it this way, but… until a company has some form of financial exit (e.g. acquisition or IPO), you are really more like a donor than an investor! Think of it this way: since there is no liquidity in early stage company stock, you can't sell the stock and recoup any of your original investment. You're stuck with stock that, for all intents and purposes, has no financial value that you can monetize. As Christopher likes to point out, equity from investors is like a loan the <u>buyer</u> of your company will pay back.

As part of your due diligence research, you will need to understand how the company will achieve liquidity through a financial exit for the investors. Since 95%+ of exits with technology companies are through acquisition, the most important questions will revolve around who the potential buyers are and why they want to buy the company. The following questions are important to review with the company during the diligence process. That said, there are other topics related to exits that you should become familiar with. Let's start with the following introduction.

Q

Ham, help us understand what a potential buyer looks for when they are looking to make acquisitions. What are some of the scenarios we should think about?

When you decide to invest in an early stage company, you are primarily investing because you believe you will make a good financial return on your investment. In most cases (and please note that I said "most" and not "all"), when a company makes an acquisition, it's because they believe it will produce a good financial return for their business. There are numerous scenarios where a large company makes an acquisition, but the following 5 cases are the ones that create the most value for the acquirer.

- A new product that complements a fast growing product line of a large company

- A disruptive product that has the potential to damage a larger company's market position or become difficult to "sell around"

- A new product that fills a newly emerging gap in a big company's product line

- A new product with strategic patents that a buyer cannot risk having fall into a competitor's hands

- A new product that is clearly constrained by lack of sales and would be instantly accretive and profitable in the hands of a larger sales force.

This list is not exhaustive, but it does cover the outcomes that will produce some of the greatest returns to investors. One type of acquisition that isn't listed above is the situation where a company is acquired for the team. These so-called "acqui-hires" might produce a good financial return for the company founders (especially if the buyer creates a "carve-out" from the proceeds to be paid directly to the team as an inducement for doing the deal), but they rarely turn out to be great returns for the early stage investor.

Q

How do you determine who the likely buyers are and why they would buy the company?

First off, we expect the company will pull together an initial list of likely candidates. As part of an investor presentation, the CEO should discuss potential buyers and accompany this discussion with a brief explanation describing why each type of buyer would be interested. For example, if you are looking to invest in a data analytics company that tracks consumer behavior, potential buyers could include the following:

- Large enterprise software companies (e.g. Oracle, SAP, IBM)

- Consulting firms with analytics practices (e.g. McKinsey, Bain, BCG)

- Consumer data analytics companies (e.g. Nielsen, ComScore)

Sometimes there are many types of buyers and it takes some thought to figure out which might be the one best-positioned to pay top dollar for your startup. Let's take an example.

Imagine a hypothetical supplier of cutting edge new technology to the trucking industry. The most obvious category of buyer which leaps immediately to mind might be a customer of the technology who would like to use the technology in their fleet (and keep it out of their competitors' fleets). But what they will be able to pay is going to face a natural cap that is a function of their limited market share. In effect they can only pay you in proportion to the number of trucks they can reasonably expect to ever use it on.

So you could widen your aperture and look for a broader category of buyer. How about selling to one of the truck manufacturers? That is an improvement because there are fewer of them, and each is bigger than any given fleet operator of trucks. But they each still only control a piece of the market - let's say there are five and they each control 20% of the market. They might be hungry to buy to keep their competitors from getting the technology, but each of them only controls a fraction of the market. Your technology is universal and can be used market wide. The value of your company is much greater than an individual manufacturer can justify paying - it could apply to the whole market, and yet a 20% market share holder cannot pay for the full market.

As part of an investor presentation, the CEO should discuss potential buyers and accompany this discussion with a brief explanation describing why each type of buyer would be interested.

So maybe you need to go even broader still and you look at, say, telematics and electronics makers. They sell to all the truck manufacturers, so that is good, but upon inspection, you realize there are many different kinds of solutions in this market, and none of them has a business as massive as even one single truck manufacturer. So even though they serve the entire market across all manufacturers, none of them is really that big because there are so many different categories of product in the telematics and electronics market.

So you scratch your head and start over by asking yourself "who has a huge business selling to this entire industry and might be interested in our safety-related product?" With some research you learn that there are only two manufacturers of brakes for big trucks. They are both huge companies, they are fiercely competitive with each other, and they are very hungry for ways to differentiate their commodity brakes as a much more comprehensive "total safety solution."

Now, you might have found your ideal buyer! It took some digging and some thinking, but that is what diligence is all about. In doing the research and thinking about how things might play out, you can get a much better handle on the natural maximum potential value of the company. Figuring that out might make you more, or less interested in the deal, but either way, isn't the effort worth it?

In my view, this kind of analysis should be an important part of the investor pitch because it shows how well the CEO understands their market and the overall ecosystem they live in.

> You should ask buyers about key milestones they are looking for before they are willing to make a serious acquisition offer. Sometimes the milestones are product stage-based and sometimes they are company revenue-based.

Next, starting with the 5 most likely acquisition scenarios from the above question, you should be able to add to the company's initial list of buyers and reasons for buying. In certain cases, we will work with some of our contacts in the Investment Banking industry to help us with this research. Investment Bankers with an M&A practice are always talking to large companies and are a great source of market intelligence.

Q

When would they buy the company? What milestones does the company need to achieve before an acquisition is likely?

There is no shortcut for finding an answer to these questions. And, you can't base a decision on gut feeling. This is where industry expertise is critical. Unless you or your colleagues have deep experience in the market, you will have to reach out to potential buyers to answer these questions. Or, once again, you can speak to an Investment Banker with contacts at the potential buyers.

You should ask buyers about key milestones they are looking for before they are willing to make a serious acquisition offer. Sometimes the milestones are product stage-based and sometimes they are company revenue-based. Examples of key milestones might be:

- Getting FDA approval for a medical device company

- Building an installed base of 10,000,000 users for a consumer-focused startup

- Getting to $10M in Annual Recurring Revenue for an enterprise software company

Q

Once those milestones are achieved, what's a likely acquisition price?

That's the $64,000,000 question! Wouldn't we all love to know what that number will be ahead of time. It would make our lives so much easier. The good news here is that there should be some recent data that you can base your answers on. In almost all cases, there are prior acquisitions that you can use for comparison purposes. If you can't find at least 2 or 3 similar types of acquisitions made within the past few years, I'd be surprised. And, lack of acquisitions might be a sign that there isn't much buying activity going on in the company's market segment.

So, once again, this is an area where having deep industry experience either on the company's founding team, your investment group, or through investment banking connections is needed.

> Having deep industry experience either on the company's founding team, your investment group, or through investment banking connections is needed.

Q

Explain some more about these different categories of acquisitions you alluded to. Why is it important to understand these categories?

A few years ago, Launchpad initiated a research project to better understand how exits worked in the world of technology companies. One of Christopher and my colleagues, Bob Gervis, put together a well thought out overview for Launchpad that categorized exits into the following buckets:

- **Buy the Team** - Company has limited if any intrinsic value beyond the knowledge and experience of the team. Acquirer's objective is to hire the people (i.e Acqui-Hire).

- **Buy the Technology** - Company has some Intellectual Property (IP) in addition to the knowledge and experience of the team. Acquirer's objective is to hire the people and obtain control of the IP.

- **Buy the Feature** - Company's technology has some proven capability, but has achieved limited market acceptance. Acquirer is adding a "feature" to its existing product line along with the people who created the IP.

- **Buy the Product** - Company has built a product with early market acceptance and they are nearing product/market fit. Acquirer is buying a product with some traction that they can apply significant sales and marketing resources to and increase growth.

Buy the Business - Company has built a viable, profitable stand-alone business that is centered around one product or a series of closely-related products. Acquirer views this as the purchase of a growth business with the intent of accelerating the growth and increasing profitability.

So, why is it important to understand these categories? Well, if you understand the ultimate buyer's motivations, you will gain insight into both the potential valuation of the company and the likelihood of its occurrence. As you might expect, a buyer will pay a lot more when they are "Buying a Business" vs. "Buying a Team".

There are many different variables in calculating the actual price a buyer will pay when making an acquisition. We tend to use the following guidelines as we are making our estimates. These guidelines are based on our past experience, which by no means should be considered based on exhaustive research. So take these numbers with a grain of salt.

- **Buy the Team** - Relatively quick exit (investor return: < 1.5x)

- **Buy the Technology** - Relatively quick exit (investor return: 0.5x to 2x)

- **Buy the Feature** - Intermediate term exit (investor return: 1x to 4x)

- **Buy the Product** - Intermediate term exit (investor return: 4x to 8x)

- **Buy the Business** - Long term exit (investor return: 5x to 20x+)

Chapter 12

The Fine Print - Deal Terms and Payoff

As the diligence process proceeds towards conclusion, thoughts naturally turn to the terms of the deal. Regardless of whether there is an existing term sheet to review, or a need to negotiate and establish a set of terms for the deal, thought needs to be given to the terms of the deal. Just like the various risks reviewed in diligence, deal terms can have a huge impact on the outcome of an investment.

The findings from the diligence process will inform the deal terms in two ways. First, important risks may need to be addressed by extra emphasis on specific deal terms. Second, the learnings about the company's anticipated capital path and likely exit scenarios will inform the approach taken with terms relating to deal economics.

All deal terms can be grouped into four categories, and each of them can be used to address specific aspects of the diligence findings:

1. **Deal Economics** - Investors want to make sure they get a big enough slice of the pie to make the investment worthwhile on a risk-adjusted basis. They want to make sure they get paid back first. They want to put a time-clock on the founders. And they want to make sure employee options don't dilute them inappropriately.

2. **Investor Rights / Protection** - Investors want to make sure no future financing deals contain terms which unduly diminish the value of their investment or lead to someone moving into a superior liquidity position (without

paying appropriately for that right).

3. **Governance, Management & Control** - Investors want to know what's going on in the company, have a say in critical decisions, and protect against founder behavior that could be damaging to the company.

4. **Exit/Liquidity** - Investors want to make sure they maximize the chances to get their money back in all possible exit scenarios (positive or negative), even if they have to force such a situation to occur.

Q

Christopher, where do you start when approaching deal terms in the diligence context?

Deal economics are always the starting point because, if you cannot make the deal work from an economic standpoint, nothing else matters much. When establishing deal terms, obviously the pre-money valuation matters a great deal because it drives how large a piece of the company you start out with, which is the foundation of your returns. It is important to pay attention to the fine print in deal economics, however, because beyond the issue of **pre-money valuation**, there are a number of terms that really drive returns.

> Far too many start-ups run into trouble because they let their valuation get away from them in the early rounds. They end up being unable to raise money in later rounds without a very damaging down round because their valuation becomes unattractive relative to the progress they've made.

But let's start with valuation. If you get the valuation wrong (as in, too high), you are really hurting yourself in two ways:

- Your out-right return multiple will naturally be lower even if the company succeeds, because you received a smaller stake for your investing dollar, but

- Less obviously, you may also be significantly reducing the chances of the company even succeeding at all.

Far too many start-ups run into trouble because they let their valuation get away from them in the early rounds. They end up being unable to raise money in later rounds without a very damaging down round because their valuation becomes unattractive relative to the progress they've made. So they struggle to raise, are over-shopped and pick up a "company in trouble" stigma, and then ultimately have no option other than to try to do a cram-down at a lower price. Best case, such a cram-down badly hurts all the early supporters of the company (most critically the founders). But that's the best case - in most cases the company doesn't ever recover and ends up failing.

Thus, getting the valuation right is job one.

Another very basic driver of returns is your **liquidation preference**, which is your right to get paid before common stockholders. It can be expressed as a 1X which gives you the right to get one times your money back, or as a 2x or 3X or higher. Your diligence findings will inform how you approach this clause in particular. Every term that early stage investors ask for, later stage investors will feel entitled to, and this one can have a multiplying effect on the size of the preference stack, which very directly affects your returns, particularly in less than home-run situations. There are a lot of good reasons to avoid multiple liquidation preferences and instead stick with a 1X.

So if you are going with a 1X liquidation preference, the main question is whether to go with participating preferred stock or not. Suffice it to say that participating preferred will have better investor economics in mediocre outcomes, provided the company does not go on to raise several additional rounds from investors who also demand

participating preferred. In bad outcomes and home run outcomes, participating preferred won't make an enormous difference in your returns.

The **option pool** is another term very much driven by diligence fact-finding. How many shares are needed in the option pool is a function of what advisors and senior team members still need to be added, in addition to what the hiring plan looks like during the milestone period covered by the round. Option pool sizing obviously affects the company's ability to attract and retain talent, but it can also affect returns pretty significantly because it has a major impact on valuation. If the pool is established prior to investment, that is equivalent to a lower valuation, and if it is established after investment, that is the dilution equivalent of a higher valuation.

Depending on the structure and experience of the team, **protective provisions**, which give investors some say in decision-making, can also be important protections. In this category you will find things like board seats which ensure investors information and control, as well as approval rights, which allow a class of investors to have a say in future financings.

The other terms worth paying close attention to at this stage are **participation rights** in future financings, which give you the ability to double-down when a company starts to look like a winner, and exit options like **co-sale rights** and **drag-along rights** to help force exits and partial exits when things are kind of stuck. If you are dealing with a founding team whose members have different experience levels or economic situations, making sure you have a solid drag along to force a consensus may be the difference between getting a mediocre return and no return at all.

One frequently-overlooked term is the **dividend**. If your diligence suggests that the market size may not be huge or you fear the team is cautious and may move more slowly and deliberately than average, you could be looking at a very long holding period for your stock. In these cases, having a dividend accumulating in the background can make an enormous difference in returns. For example, using the rule of 72, an 8% dividend alone will give you a 2X if left to run for 9 years.

Q

Of those deal economic terms, which should be the priority? Which has the greatest real-world effect on angel returns?

Many people would say that the initial valuation you pay (and the resulting size of your stake) is the most important. And valuation is very important, but if you study the way a typical portfolio works, it is clear that the rare big winners really drive the majority of your returns, so I could make a great case that there is no term more important than participation rights in future financings. If you have the ability to double and triple down into a huge win as it is taking off, the importance of that right will dwarf all the other rights in all the other deals put together.

> If you study the way a typical portfolio works, it is clear that the rare big winners really drive the majority of your returns, so I could make a great case that there is no term more important than participation rights in future financings.

In more normal companies delivering solid but not spectacular returns, your liquidation preferences, your protective provisions and your drag-along rights might end up being the most important. And in some minority of cases, your anti-dilution protection might matter, though as I have noted, few companies go on to survive down rounds.

Q

If Diligence is about getting to know the team, do you look for extra control in cases where some or all of the founders seem strong-willed?

This is where the terms on governance, management and control are important. These terms don't actually vary as much as you might think, however. In an extraordinary situation you might seek some extra control, but typical preferred stock investing terms give most of the day-to-day control of the company to the board of directors, and reserve approval of really major decisions (such as M&A transactions) and really economically impactful decisions (such as issuing more stock for another financing) to some or all classes of shareholders. So in the real world what you typically see is that the board negotiates and approves the typical M&A transaction but the actual deal documents require shareholder approval before the final close. Since the directors are closest to the situation and they have legal duties to act in the best interests of the shareholders, it is pretty rare to see a situation with young companies where the board approves and recommends a transaction and the shareholders disagree. Thus, as you are completing your diligence and thinking about who to put on the board, you are obviously making a very important decision.

Individual shareholders are typically not going to be able to block a transaction they disagree with unless they have such a large stake in the company that they can prevent a majority from being reached by other means. As part of your diligence, you should pay close attention the capitalization of the company - both before and after giving effect to the financing. If there are particular issues to be concerned about, for example, a departed founder who has some grievances, you should consider making adjustments to the capitalization of the company or the terms of the voting agreement. For example, you might enlarge the option pool beyond the normal size and grant some of that stock to the CEO, or , as a condition of investment, you might take extra

care to require all the founders to agree to voting provisions and drag-along clauses which stipulate that they will vote with the will of the majority of the preferred stockholders.

Q

Where your diligence raises specific concerns about the team's commitment to an exit, are there things you can do? For example are there deal terms that might allow investors to force an exit?

Yes there are. The most common, reasonable and egalitarian provision is the drag-along right, which requires the minority to vote with the majority when an exit opportunity is on the table. Other common forcing functions favoring smaller classes of investors include debt maturity dates and redemption rights windows, which both tend to require an exit (or a refinancing) to provide the liquidity necessary to meet the payment or redemption obligation.

Less common, but equally effective (some might say equally destructive) is the demand dividend, which can be structured to allow a class of shareholders to demand a cash pay-out proportional to their shareholdings. If demand dividends and redemption rights provisions are not carefully structured with some balance and some protections, they can be like giving one class of shareholder the right to pull the pin out of the grenade at will, based solely on what is good for that class (i.e. VC fund expiration date or the like) without regard to what is best for the company or the other shareholders. Arguably, if your diligence finds issues so significant that you feel you need very strong terms to remedy them, you might want to revisit whether the deal is a good idea in the first place.

The golden rule in investing is the last round to bring the gold generally makes the rules, so it is important to ensure everyone is on the same page before co-investing.

Q

What about situations where your diligence raises concerns that the team wants to flip the company to the first buyer they can find or accept an "acqui-hire" deal? Are there deal terms that might allow investors to block an exit?

Yes. The most common are (i) the right to appoint board directors and (ii) clauses which fall under the heading of protective provisions (which are also sometimes called "negative covenants"). Protective provisions can require super-majorities on board votes or shareholder votes; may require certain decisions to go to the board or to a class of stock; or may reserve approval/veto rights for certain directors or certain classes of stock.

Q

What about capital intensity? Are their terms that you should pay extra attention to if your diligence suggests a company is going to need a lot of capital?

This is where the investor rights and protection clauses are important. Investors want to make sure no future financing deals contain terms which unduly diminish the value of their investment or lead to someone moving into a superior liquidity position (without paying appropriately for that right). In situations where a company is going to be needing to raise significant capital, you need to look carefully at the terms that allow you to control future financing rounds.

Why is this so important? Because VCs coming in after angels may end up in a position to block an exit that would be a great return for founders and angels. Why would they do that? Because VC economics are different from angel economics. VCs are generally running large funds and are required to distribute returned capital to limited partners. An exit that provides a really good return to founders or early shareholders (who have typically been waiting longer), might not be such a good return for the VC who came in at a much higher valuation. They may have a strong preference for instead putting more money in and going for more aggressive growth before selling. This not only gives them more management fees on the newly invested money, but it also gives them a greater chance of having an exit with enough scale to "move the needle" in terms of their overall fund returns.

This dichotomy of perspectives is a classic illustration of the dangers of mixing different kinds of investors. During the due diligence period before investing, angels should always consider how much capital a company is likely to need, where it is likely going to come from, and how it is going to be staged in over time. The golden rule in investing is the last round to bring the gold generally makes the rules, so it is important to ensure everyone is on the same page before co-investing.

Chapter 13

Getting On The Same Page - Verifying Goal Alignment

Have you ever been disappointed by someone or by some product that you purchased? Nine times out of ten it's due to not having the right expectations for one reason or another. Investments are no different from other purchases. If you are not clear on what you are getting yourself into, buyer's remorse usually results. In early stage investing, we use a term to describe setting expectations... it's called "Goal Alignment".

So what do we mean by this term? Goal Alignment is typically used to establish common ground around the long range plans of the company. It's crucial to make sure the investors and the founders are in sync and want and expect the same things. Goal Alignment needs to cover a variety of areas, including:

- Long term company objectives

- Use of funds and aggressiveness of investment levels

- Long range financing plans and assumptions

- Exit strategies and expectations on size and timing

During the due diligence process, you will spend a fair amount of time interacting with the CEO. This is an important time to establish the basis for a working relationship between you and the CEO. You should use this time period to have pointed discussions around long term goals for the company. Hopefully, your expectations and the CEO's expectations will be in alignment. Goal alignment is not a "set it and forget it" proposition. Your goals

may be in sync at the time you invest, but you will need to check in on a regular basis to ensure they stay in alignment!

> Goal Alignment is typically used to establish common ground around the long range plans of the company.

Q

Ham, in a startup company, cash is always tight, so alignment on goals and spending priorities is paramount. What financial topics do you frequently discuss with the CEO during diligence?

One of the first conversations I have with the CEO revolves around where and how fast the company is planning to spend the cash we are investing. This "Use of Funds" discussion presents an interesting test for our early working relationship. Are we in alignment on issues such as compensation for the management team, key initial hires and marketing spend? Do we agree on what we need to learn about product / market fit before we pour on the gas? Is there a consensus about how many new markets we will enter simultaneously? (One can only imagine what those conversations must have been like at Uber, which has raised tens of billions to go on a spree to hire and enter every major market globally all at once. If you were not prepared for that, the dilution associated with raising that much capital, even at Uber's valuation might come as somewhat of a surprise.)

Management compensation is often the most difficult financial/spending conversation you will have with a CEO. Frequently, I will invest in a company where the CEO and her team have forgone salaries for the past year or so. They don't have the financial reserves to continue paying their personal expenses, and so they need to start drawing a salary as soon as the round closes. If the salary requirements fit comfortably within the amount of capital being raised, then things should be okay. For example, if the company is raising $750,000 and that allows the company to make significant progress over the next 12 months, then salaries are most likely reasonable. On the other hand, I've run into situations where the CEO expected a salary similar to what he received working for a large corporation. This salary expectation would seriously limit the company's financial plan and place key milestones at risk. Your challenge as a prospective investor is to convince the CEO that a high salary is not in the best interests of either the company or their personal future financial success if it means trading off a lot of their stock to get it.

Q

What other questions should you discuss with the CEO during diligence?

Another set of alignment-oriented questions might be along the lines of:

- What are the growth milestones that allow the company to raise a future round of financing at a favorable valuation to the early investors?

- Will there be enough funding from this early round to allow the company to achieve these important growth milestones?

Within every industry there are key milestones that allow a company to raise capital from different stages of investor. For example, in the software world, seed stage investors like to see a company that has a shipping product and a few paying customers. The next stage of investors like to see somewhere between $100K and $250K of Monthly Recurring Revenue (MRR).

> Make sure you and the CEO set realistic expectations on what the company will achieve with the newly raised funding.

And finally, growth stage investors like to see upwards of $1M in MRR and a well defined set of growth metrics. Compare these milestones to those in the life sciences. Biotech and Medical Device companies tend to have milestones that are based on successful clinical outcomes, first in animal and then in human trials. Every industry is different. It's important for investors and company founders to have a deep understanding of what those milestones are and how they should be applied to their company.

Assuming you are in agreement on key milestones, your next challenge is to make sure they are achievable in the timeframe and on the budget the CEO presents to you. We all know that entrepreneurs are optimists and this optimism usually results in missed schedules and over-budget projects. So keep this in mind as you scrub the company financial plan. Make sure you and the CEO set realistic expectations on what the company will achieve with the newly raised funding.

Q

Early stage investors participate during the first round or two of a company's financing history. Why should early stage investors worry about a company's long range financing plan?

Early stage investors need to understand a company's long range funding plan so they can answer several key diligence questions:

- **What is the Financing Risk**: Does the company need to raise capital from investors with deeper pockets than the early stage investors? If so, how likely is it for the company to attract these investors?

- **What is the Timeline to Exit**: If there are many additional rounds of financing after this round, how will that impact the time before an exit occurs?

- **What are the Expected Returns:** How will the dilution created by any future rounds of financing affect the returns of the early stage investor?

In general, I prefer to invest in capital efficient businesses because they tend to have a greater variety of exit options, including some with faster times to exit. So it's important that I work with the founders to develop a realistic long term funding plan that will lead to a profitable exit for both the early stage investors and the founders. However, it's not unusual to have two alternate funding strategies: one that leads to an early exit and requires minimal capital and another that builds a large company over many years and requires significant amounts of outside funding. Make sure the investors and the CEO agree on the point at which the decision will be made and understand the risks and rewards for each strategy.

Topics relating to financing are the biggest issues related to Goal Alignment. They tend to be the most contentious between investor and entrepreneur. Hopefully, you can keep an open dialogue so things don't resemble a pair of spouses arguing over their household finances.

> It's not unusual to have two alternate funding strategies: one that leads to an early exit and requires minimal capital and another that builds a large company over many years and requires significant amounts of outside funding.

the type of sales strategy can have a massive impact on the expense structure and capital intensity of a company, so it should be discussed. However, keep in mind that for your views and opinions on these topics to have credibility, you must have real product/industry knowledge you can share with the entrepreneur. Having productive discussions on these topics before you invest will help you to better understand the CEO's thinking process. And, it will set the stage for future conversations during board meetings and strategy sessions.

Q

Are there other topics you like to review in Goal Alignment?

Yes, there are secondary topics that are important to discuss with the entrepreneur during the diligence process. Two areas that I like to cover include Product Strategy and Go-to-Market Strategy. For example,

Q

What are some goal alignment disasters leading to disappointments for early stage investors?

The biggie? Not making money on your investment! Here are two examples of how this can happen. In both cases the entrepreneur achieves the result they were looking for and the investor doesn't.

Example 1 (Acqui-Hire): A young entrepreneur and her team build an awesome product in a hot market. They start shipping the product and get an early acquisition offer. They sell the company for $5M one year after they raise $1M from the early stage investors. They walk away with $3.5M in their pockets. Not bad for a couple of 25 year old founders. The investors end up with $1.5M and make a 50% return on their investment. The founders are happy because they made some quick money early in their career, and they are getting high paying jobs with a big company. What a great notch in their belts. The investors, on the other hand, walk away with a small return on an opportunity that had tremendous potential. This company had the potential to be a 10X or 20X return. Instead, it was a 1.5X return. Better than a sharp stick in the eye, but not what you were hoping for.

Example 2 (Lifestyle Business): A seasoned executive starts a company midway through his career. After raising $4M from investors over a few rounds of financing, the business starts to gain real traction. The company gets to cash flow breakeven, but it's not generating much profit. Growth is modest at 10% per year. The CEO is drawing a nice salary in the range of $250K annually, and is satisfied with his financial and work situation. He enjoys being the CEO of a tech company and doesn't want to sell the business. The company has become the dreaded "lifestyle business." There is no easy way for an investor to get their money out of the company, and any chance of a 10X return are pretty much eliminated.

> The type of sales strategy can have a massive impact on the expense structure and capital intensity of a company, so it should be discussed.

Exit strategies need to be discussed with the founders early on. Do they want to flip the company in a few

111

years or are they building a big business? And, make sure they are not looking for a lifestyle business! Starting the exit strategy discussion early on is an important part of setting up the company (and investors) for success. Startups rarely survive without being a part of a larger ecosystem and it's this ecosystem that plays the central role in an exit.

Chapter 14

Learning the Hard Way - Due Diligence Mistakes

It is easy to talk about due diligence in the abstract, but it is much harder to practice what you preach. One of the hardest things about early stage investing is that it is really risky - if you don't have some suspension of disbelief, and you obsess too much about cataloging every risk, you will never get a deal done.

On some level you need to accept the fact that:

- Every early stage company will have some warts

- Things will happen that cannot be foreseen

- A significant portion of your investments will be unsuccessful no matter what you do

- It is necessary to put some trust in great teams and the power of shared benefit alignment that comes with equity investing

- Sometimes you just have to take a deep breath and jump into the water.

Given that leaps of faith are necessary, mistakes are bound to happen. One has to be somewhat philosophical and roll with the punches. Christopher likes to use humor in these situations, pointing out that "experience is what you get when you don't get what you want." Or asking "you are investing in a young team you've just met, with an unproven product in a market that does not yet exist. What could possibly go wrong?"

As a way of wrapping up this book with a review, let's take a look at a few common mistakes and see what we can learn from them.

> Given that leaps of faith are necessary, mistakes are bound to happen. One has to be somewhat philosophical and roll with the punches.

Q

Christopher can you describe a really big issue you missed during the diligence process that ended up coming back to bite you when the investment failed a few years down the road?

The most painful issues I missed have clustered around two core areas:

(i) Confusing likability or prior accomplishments on the part of an entrepreneur with the competence needed to pull off the current task. I've lost money with entrepreneurs who are great guys or great gals and had accomplished good things in their prior career endeavors, but were completely over their heads and unable to adapt when driving the new opportunity. As a result, I try to think hard about not what skills are required now, but what skills the coming opportunity will require down the road, and make sure the entrepreneur has, or is willing and able to get, those particular skills.

(ii) Confusing early adopter excitement with true market pull. It has been said that "anybody can get the first 10% of a market" and Geoffrey Moore's Crossing the Chasm stands for that proposition, but the key to growing a company is finding a big enough market of willing buyers who can be accessed in an affordable way (relative to their lifetime value). The product may be good, and there may be lots of people who might buy it, but unfortunately a company's true market is limited to those customers for whom that purchase is a top pain point and a top buying priority. Often a marginal improvement on a marginal cost is not enough to drive buying behavior in all but the earliest of adopters. So the key is to recognize when you are looking at what is sometimes called false traction and do some further digging. There is no substitute for talking to real customers and prospects before doing the deal in these situations.

Q

Ham: what are some mistakes you have made that related to your evaluation of the business and the plan?

Well… that's a really long list, and will make for a great book some time in the near future! So, I will keep my answer short and simple with a couple of examples.

The first mistake I will highlight relates to timing. The gist of the issue focuses on the question, **"Is this the right time for this idea?"**

Many times I've been impressed by a CEO's ability to spin a great story of how her company will change the world. They build a great product and it demos well. Prospective customers love the prototype. But, if the company relies on others to provide a key part of their product/ service (e.g. high speed broadband or long lasting batteries), and that key part doesn't exist, then the company will fail. So make sure that the CEO understands what the whole product solution needs to look like and has a credible plan to deliver it.

> A savvy CEO (and investor) will make sure that they are selling a product that solves one of the top 2 or 3 problems that the target customer has.

The second mistake relates to an incomplete understanding of the dynamics in your target market. At Launchpad, we've invested in several companies that built products for the restaurant industry. The products work well and they solve a real problem. Unfortunately, the problem is not high on the restaurant owner's priority list. In other words, the company is selling aspirin, not oxygen. A savvy CEO (and investor) will make sure that they are selling a product that solves one of the top 2 or 3 problems that the target customer has.

Q

Christopher, what are some mistakes you have made with your evaluation of the team?

The worst diligence mistake I've ever made in the team area had to do with taking someone else's word for it. It was a large and splashy deal with a lot of investor momentum and the CEO was pretty polished. Two groups claimed to have done significant diligence, and had written reports. So we based our decision on those reports and the time we spent with the CEO. Because they were from a neighboring state, we never met the rest of the team. Turns out the CEO really didn't have much control because there were huge personality issues and undisclosed in-law relationships at the company. Predictably, the company was clumsy, slow and indecisive and failed to change its strategy in time to save itself. The CEO was happy to listen to investor input, and seemed to understand it, but was basically powerless to really drive an agenda. That company took several million in angel dollars with it to its grave.

Another mistake I have made a couple times is what I will call the "grown up supervision" mistake. You invest in a company in part because you are reassured that they have already brought in an experienced pro who has been to the rodeo before. You figure, this is very refreshing - here is a team that is self-aware enough to know they need a real CEO. The hired-gun CEO is great at raising money and has a good resume, but as things unfold, it becomes clear that he is not very good - or at least not good at the things this young company

needs. Perhaps the CEO took the job because he was washed out or burned out in his career, or perhaps he didn't want to work hard enough at the startup, or perhaps he didn't have founder-like passion for the company's mission, or perhaps the chemistry between him and the founders wasn't great. Regardless of the reason, the company predictably never gels, there is no esprit de corps, the commitment levels are low and the tensions are high and the company just cannot zig and zag fast enough to adapt to its reality. It is flat-footed, befuddled and increasingly embattled. And of course the company's demise is hastened by the cash drain of having to pay a mid-career executive with a mortgage and a picket fence.

Ham, what's a mistake you have made with the investment itself?

As an angel investor, I get to look at companies at a very early stage. Sometimes, I really like the CEO, but I want to see more progress before I pull the trigger and make an initial investment. In most cases, waiting hasn't been a problem because the company came back to me a year later and I invested then. But... there have been two cases where I took a pass the first time around, and I regret my decision to this day. In those two cases, each company made tremendous progress with their seed financing. When they went back to raise additional capital, large VCs lead the round and didn't allow any new investors to join the round. Both companies went on to achieve great exits for their investors. So based on these two experiences, I changed my approach. Now, when I really like the team, I tend to invest a small amount so that I am on the Cap Table and have rights to invest additional funds in future rounds.

Q

Christopher, what are some mistakes you have made when evaluating possible exits and planning for exits?

The biggest mistake with exits is not establishing with certainty that the team is focused on exits, and understands that they are driving toward one someday, and that they know the steps and the path they need to go down. Too many companies end up in comfortable situations where the company growth slows and the company drifts along while paying the management team nice salaries and holding the investors' money hostage. It is easy to see how it happens because once a CEO builds a business with $5-10M in revenue, the weaker ones can start to feel conservative, like there is something real at risk in undertaking daring strategic shifts in search of growth, and they doubt their ability to pull it off or they fear they will never have it this good again or never get another CEO job again, so they just drift. I am not a fan of redemption rights windows, but in recent years I have started to favor using an accumulating dividend on the preferred in deals with smaller more mature markets where there is a greater possibility of that happening. It can at least put management's feet to the fire knowing the value of the company's equity is slowly shifting to investors over time. The other thing I focus

118

on more now is making sure the board keeps exits top of mind all the time.

The next biggest mistake is lack of diligence on the terms of a specific exit opportunity. You are impatient to exit so without thinking it through, you end up agreeing to take private company stock and/or agreeing to an earn-out (or what I like to call seller financing!) Sometimes you have no choice, but it is almost always a disaster - very few M&A transactions are actually successful, so you have just converted your stock in a nice little company into the stock of a company that just did a bad acquisition. And they are likely going to mismanage the new business so the earn-out won't get paid. So I try to insist on at least enough cash to get the principal back and a decent return.

> The biggest mistake with exits is not establishing with certainty that the team is focused on exits, and understands that they are driving toward one someday, and that they know the steps and the path they need to go down.

Speaking of plugging your nose and accepting a marginal exit, this brings me to the third biggest mistake, which is a failure to do your diligence on market conditions and competitive pressures and passing up a relatively poor deal in the hopes of getting a better deal, and then ending up with no deal at all. Sometimes you have to be realistic and know when you are beat, and just unload the company when the chance is presented. And this is not just limited to small deals - I've seen it plenty of times in that context, but it also happens in big deals. We once sold a portfolio company to a high-flying pre-IPO company (for stock, of course) and the pre-IPO company faltered, could never get their billion-dollar IPO done, so they dithered around trying to optimize the exit for the various VCs in the deal and finally got acquired for about $400M. Buried in the disclosure documents was the fact that while they were messing around chasing their billion dollar deal, they turned down an offer of $800M. Talk about not doing enough homework to recognize when someone is handing you a life preserver...

Part Two

The Art and Science of Deal Leadership

Active deal leadership is one of the essential elements of success in early stage investing. As legendary investor Fred Wilson observed, every round needs a lead investor:

"A lead investor sets the price and terms of the investment, takes a large part of the round, and usually agrees to represent the entire round on the board. Then everyone else gets to pile in behind them and piggyback on all of that work. And the entrepreneur and lead investor allow the followers to do that because either they are likely to help the company in some way or because the company needs more capital than the lead is prepared to invest at this time."

Deal leadership is hard, and Fred Wilson doesn't even mention the diligence aspects of deal leadership. Being a great deal lead takes experience, or the guidance of a great process.

That is the purpose of this section - to provide the guidance of a great process so that more people can step up to serve as much-needed deal leads. As you work your way through this book, and the tools and checklists included as appendices, you will benefit from the learnings of very experienced investors who have honed their process over many years, and over many hundreds of deal lead efforts culminating in investments in nearly 100 companies.

Early stage investing networks can struggle with motivating members to step up and get involved in deal leadership and due diligence. Part of the issue is fear of the unknown and being overwhelmed by a sense of not knowing where to start. We put this section together in order to help people get over the hump and get involved.

Not every investor needs to be a deal lead, but every successful early stage investment has a deal lead. You cannot make money in this space without leads on deals. Do you have what it takes? Read along to find out.

Chapter 16

The Importance of Deal Leadership

The first time I served as a deal lead was unintentional. I happened upon a team I really liked, going after a market I thought was really attractive, with a solution I thought was really smart. So I started telling other investors about it. Many perked up and took an interest, but nothing was really happening because there was no bandwagon to jump onto.

The entrepreneurs had no idea how to raise money or structure a round, so they were hesitant to jump in and set terms, and the other investors, while interested, had plenty of other priorities to attend to. So if this was going to go anywhere, someone was going to need to define the round and establish an acceptable set of terms for people to invest.

> Sometimes being a deal lead is about being a cheerleader and manufacturing enthusiasm, but more often than not it is about managing that enthusiasm and defining a process.

In thinking about terms, I had a sense of where the market was at, but just the same, I spoke to the interested investors to calibrate against what they thought might be acceptable. And I spoke to the company as my thoughts came together. From there it was very natural for me to recommend a way to go about communicating those terms. They agreed. We set out a simple termsheet. We showed it to some other investors. They agreed to come on board. And looking back, I realize that in that moment, I became a deal lead for the first time.

A lot has changed over many years and many investments, but that essential core interaction has not. Every deal needs a lead, a focal point, a way to prime the pump. When I told Ham the story of that first deal leadership experience, he asked me to expand on the role a bit more. Here are his questions and my answers.

Q

Christopher, you and I have led many, many deals over the years. At a high level, what does it mean to be a deal lead?

The deal lead is the investor who steps up to take responsibility for driving the process and sets the terms on which the investment will happen. The deal lead is like the catalyst in a chemical reaction. It is the ingredient that makes the chain reaction start to happen.

Sometimes being a deal lead is about being a cheerleader and manufacturing enthusiasm, but more often than not it is about managing that enthusiasm and defining a process. From a leadership perspective, deals really have three main phases:

- Discovery

- Diligence

- Syndication

Discovery is really the "pitching" phase. It is about testing the waters and finding interest and support for the concept. The deal lead can be a very valuable shepherd during the discovery process, introducing the company around to investors who might be interested.

The diligence phase is the phase where investors try to test assumptions and gauge risks and build a pressure-tested investment hypothesis. The deal lead plays an essential role of traffic cop and coordinator in group diligence efforts.

The syndication phase comes after the initial investors have committed to the termsheet and are looking for others to fill out the round. Human nature is to procrastinate, so syndication is really about staying on people and getting them to commit. The CEO should play an important role here, too, but the deal lead is invaluable as a lead investor who can talk investor-to-investor to the people contemplating the deal.

What makes a good deal lead?

I guess at a very high level it is people skills and experience with the process. To break that down into specifics, it is:

- Knowing how to run a really good diligence process that finds the efficient balance between speed and thoroughness,

- Having an eye on the market and knowing what deal terms will be attractive to other investors,

- Having connections to investors behind you who can invest along side you,

- Knowing the right things to say so you are effective at cheerleading and coaching folks along,

- Educating and mentoring the CEO through the process,

- Staying on top of things and moving the process quickly,

- Having connections to find a value-added director who can take a board seat and oversee the investment, and

- Having a group of smart investors who can help with the due diligence.

Q

Does a deal really need a lead? What about company-led rounds where the CEO puts together a termsheet?

A round absolutely can be led by the company, and it happens quite regularly, particularly in cases of necessity. But the company-led round really presents two main sets of issues:

The first set of issues occurs at the stage of building and filling the round. Every decently-sized round needs a market-attractive termsheet and a good diligence report. If a company does not have an investor to negotiate with them and hash out a set of terms that are "at market," they will end up with something based on the termsheet of their friend's company or their lawyer's suggestions for terms. These termsheets can be spotted a mile away and often have inappropriate or off-market terms buried in them. Once a few inexperienced people have committed to those terms, they become a hassle to change and act like a big roadblock to bringing other investors in.

Company-led rounds also don't have diligence materials to offer prospective investors. Without a diligence report, the company will burn themselves out trying to "re-pitch" the company and re-answer the same sets of questions over and over, with time-consuming and not entirely convincing results. A third party diligence report is not gospel, but, like a third party termsheet negotiated at arm's-length, it does add a big measure of credibility to the round. Without this credibility, it can feel like the entrepreneur must have some kind of a flaw if they have not been able to find any investors.

The second set of issues presents itself after the round is complete. It can be summarized as a "diffusion of responsibility" issue. Company-led rounds are sometimes referred to as "party rounds," meaning all that name implies.

- Nobody is in charge,

- There is no investor representation on the board,

- No meaningful governance or oversight,

- No plan for staging capital into the company and defining milestones for the next round,

- No single investor with real skin in the game,

- No one to organize and rally investors in the face of management team issues,

- Creeping valuation issues from things like stacking convertible notes, and

- A general lack of accountability and rudderlessness.

Of course some of these party round companies get lucky, gain some traction and attract the attention and oversight of key investors later. But many do not. You can imagine what happens to those which do not.

Q

Why put in the work to be a deal lead? Why not just join rounds led by other people?

Since a round only needs one lead for its many investors, that can be a perfectly viable way to go for many investors. In fact, some investors, particularly those in well-organized networks, go their entire career without stepping up as a lead. Even if you do occasionally lead, you cannot lead everything, so it is fine to invest where a trusted co-investor leads.

The syndication phase comes after the initial investors have committed to the termsheet and are looking for others to fill out the round. Human nature is to procrastinate, so syndication is really about staying on people and getting them to commit.

The advantages to doing it yourself, however, are that you can:

- Make sure it gets done right,

- Get to know, observe and work better with the CEO,

- Make sure the deal terms work and the round fills quickly so the CEO can get back to developing the company,

- Make sure there is a good overall capital strategy for the company, and

- Put someone you trust and whom you know is good on the board.

With company "projects" you really care about, sometimes the desire to lead becomes overwhelming.

Does everyone rely on the deal lead's due diligence? Is that a safe practice?

As noted above, a third party diligence report can lend tremendous credibility to a round. It is typically shared subject to a diligence sharing "treaty" or one-off disclaimer. Sharing a report can save a ton of work for both the investors and the company, but it is not a cure-all. Unless it comes from a source you know and trust, with a process you know is consistently thorough and professional, the cautious investor is going to want to double-check some things firsthand. It is very common for investors to rely on third party diligence lock, stock and barrel, but experience has taught us that it is very smart to double check key issues like the team (with a few blind reference checks of your own) and the market (with a few calls to customers or experts more knowledgeable than yourself).

Q

So if the lead sets the terms, does that mean no one else has any input or ability to renegotiate the terms?

It is possible to tweak the terms or even change them wholesale, especially if you are bringing a lot of money to the round. This is a major hassle for all involved, and a significant risk to the company due to the possibility of lost investors or lost momentum or both. So most experienced investors try as hard as they can to look at the the terms on kind of a take-it-or-leave-it basis. Either the deal is attractive on the terms being offered, or it is not. This is an example of why the deal lead role is so important. For things to work smoothly, it is essential to get

in place at the beginning an acceptable set of terms around which investors can rally. That is what a great deal lead does.

If you have to change the terms mid-process, tremendous friction, wasted time and uncertainty ensues. In some cases it is a "tempest in a teapot" because the new terms being introduced later in the process are investor-friendly and end up being viewed as a bonus to previously committed investors. But, sometimes the existing investors think the change is a bad long-term idea, even if it is technically in their short-term interest, and so they push back on the change. When that happens, you end up with a bunch of investors negotiating and fighting amongst themselves. It quickly turns into chaos. Most investors have little patience for that and will wander off and let the loudest voice win; the theory being that there are plenty of fish in the sea and it is better to look elsewhere than to try and clean up a deal that has gotten wrapped around the axle on terms.

Best case scenario, these rounds are bumpy, unprofessional time-wasters that highlight a lack of leadership and a lack of professionalism. Worst case, they careen toward entropy and simply fall apart with everyone concluding they don't need the brain-damage.

Chapter 17

Short & Savvy: Hallmarks of A Good Deal Process

During my many years working for a large enterprise software company, I participated on dozens of due diligence teams. I had the valuable experience of sitting on both sides of the table during these projects. I ran diligence teams where my company was looking to buy other companies. And, I handled the brunt of responding to a diligence effort when my company was dealing with potential acquirers. Needless to say, it's a real challenge for both sides, and not everyone understands what it takes to run a good due diligence process.

No big surprise here, but everybody seems to want good diligence to be performed, but few seem to want to do it. Partly that's because it is work, and it requires a tolerance for ambiguity and uncertainty. Also, the many diligence processes that are not well run end up being a poor experience for the participants. So what can you do to make things run smoother?

At Launchpad we run due diligence processes on early stage companies dozens of times each year. And, we've been going at it for over 15 years! We've had ample time to think about and refine the process and to assimilate great suggestions from the smart investors who have been on our teams. We believe that the goals of a good diligence process are: efficiency, insight and informed decision-making. We think the hallmarks of a good process are:

- Speed

- Efficiency

- Conciseness

- Respect

Ham has experienced diligence from both sides of the table, as well. He raised funds for several of his software startups, and he led more diligence processes at Launchpad than he probably wants to admit. So let's put Ham on the spot for a little more perspective.

We believe that the goals of a good diligence process are: efficiency, insight and informed decision-making.

Q

Ham, what does it mean to have a process with goals of efficiency, insight and informed decision-making?

First off, we find it's critical to have a standard due diligence process that everyone on our team adheres to. If everyone on a diligence team understands up front what expectations they need to meet, it makes each person's job a bit easier.

Let me give you an example from the Launchpad playbook. Let's say your assignment is to perform reference checks for the company CEO. First off, the company provides you with a list of individuals to contact. Second, you should reach out to members on your diligence team and/or your personal contacts to see if there are any other individuals who can provide a back channel reference for the CEO. You will then contact these references and ask a series of questions based on a management assessment questionnaire (see Appendix). Having performed 3 to 5 reference calls, your job is complete after you write a very short (one or two paragraph) summary of your calls. Not bad... you finished your assignment in a few hours!

So take the above example and apply it across all of the areas that you need to cover during due diligence. Each area needs a well-defined process to make it efficient and easy to accomplish in a limited number of hours. Once you define a

consistent process, you will be amazed at how efficiently it runs. And, when every member of the team has a well-defined job, the overall experience improves for all participants.

That leads us to the second part of your question relating to insight and informed decision-making. Having invested in 100+ companies over the past 15 years, we've seen lots of companies succeed and lots of companies fail. Using our post-mortem reviews on these companies, we've been able to go back and refine our due diligence checklist to make sure we are covering critical issues that can lead to either success or failure with our investments.

Let's make this concept a bit more concrete. A few years ago, after doing a review of some of our failed investments, we realized we weren't asking enough probing questions related to customer demand. When we performed customer reference checks, we usually received positive feedback from the early customers. Where we fell short in our diligence was with our understanding of customer demand beyond those early customers. This insight forced us to revise our customer reference check questionnaire (see Appendix.) Now we ask a couple of new questions during the reference check that are intended to better understand demand through the lens of buying priorities:

- On your list of the top problems in your organization, where does solving this problem fall on your priority list?

- Is your company generally an early or late adopter of new solutions?

By running a consistent, efficient diligence process that is informed by our prior investment outcomes, we believe we are making more thoughtful investment decisions. In turn, this helps to set a standard for excellence within the early stage investment community.

> Each area needs a well-defined process to make it efficient and easy to accomplish in a limited number of hours. Once you define a consistent process, you will be amazed at how efficiently it runs.

Q

When you talk about the hallmarks of a good process you cite "speed" as the first thing. What does that mean, and how do you do it?

At Launchpad, we have a bit of an advantage when it comes to the speed of our diligence efforts. A typical diligence team at Launchpad will have 8 to 15 people. We divide the diligence tasks across the group.

We always break it up into very focused assignments. Sometimes we will assign one person to a focused task and sometimes two people.

Our goal is to have the diligence process complete and at least a first draft report written within a month of starting the process. With a volunteer group of investors, this timeframe is only possible if we have different teams work in parallel on their separate tasks. We don't always achieve our one month completion goal, but we are usually close. Sometimes we are delayed by holidays and travel. Other times, we are delayed when the company is not able to get us materials in a timely manner.

Q

How about "efficiency?" How do you run a meandering, discovery-oriented process efficiently?

We discussed the answer to this question during the initial question. Ultimately, it comes down to not allowing the process to meander too far. You do this by putting in standard procedures for almost every task, and a clear focus around the expected deliverables. If you arm your diligence team with the tools they need to get the job done and you show them exactly what they are expected to produce, the resulting process can be both professional and efficient.

Q

Why do you say "conciseness," rather than "thorough?" At first blush, wouldn't you be aiming for thorough?

Thorough is a very slippery slope. Some investors want to dot every "i" and cross every "t". If we did that at Launchpad, we would end up making fewer investments. This would badly undermine the diversification so necessary to generate good angel returns, and we would burn out the folks doing the diligence. It just doesn't make sense with an early stage company to look under every rock for a problem.

Instead, you should focus on identifying the key risks that are actually likely to affect outcomes and limit your diligence to the critical areas that need further examination. So, for example, if a company has been in business for a year or so and has only a few customers, you won't spend much time looking at their prior year financials. Conversely, if the company has licensed core technology from a university, you want to make sure that the IP agreements are in order.

The resulting due diligence report should also be concise. At Launchpad, we use a Due Diligence Report Template (see Appendix.) The template is focused on 11 major topics that should be researched and understood when performing due diligence on an early stage technology company. Experience conducting hundreds of diligence projects and leading dozens and dozens of syndications has taught us that it's important to be succinct in your diligence summary. Otherwise, you will end up with a long report that investors won't read through,

thus defeating the purpose of the report.

> You should focus on identifying the key risks that are actually likely to affect outcomes and limit your diligence to the critical areas that need further examination.

Q

And where did you come up with "respect" of all things? Isn't the point to turn a skeptical and jaded eye on the claims of management and see if they are what they are cracked up to be? What does respect have to do with it?

In my view, respect is one of the core principles that guide how I conduct myself in business and in life. Therefore we insist that it be an unwavering hallmark of our organization - in all situations, and without exception. Not only is it the right thing to do, it is good business. Great teams have choice in picking investors, and they want to work with investors who respect them.

That does not mean you need to tip-toe around. It's okay to be demanding during the diligence process. A CEO should expect to answer tough questions. At that same time, the CEO should expect to be treated in a respectful manner.

And, this goes both ways. Members of the due diligence team should be treated with respect, as well. Although the startup community seems to be a large and rapidly expanding world, in reality, it's quite small. CEOs talk to other CEOs. Investors talk to other investors. It doesn't take long for a disrespectful individual to lose credibility in the community. And deservedly so, in our view.

Q

How unique is this process? How did you arrive at it?

I don't believe that our process is entirely unique. Perhaps at the detail level, but in terms of broad themes, we are probably typical of a well-run process. VCs and angels have been investing for decades. Well-run organizations have put in place processes that work well for their particular ecosystem. What we've built at Launchpad works for us because it is based on lots of:

- Deals,

- Experience,

- Observations about what works and what doesn't, and

- Great suggestions from many smart people on many smart teams.

And finally, we ask the entrepreneurs for feedback on how things went for them. It's amazing what you can learn when you ask questions!

Q

How do entrepreneurs react to it?

Many assume that it is like root canal surgery for entrepreneurs. In fact, the opposite is true. Good entrepreneurs will get a lot out of a well-designed diligence process.

- They learn a lot about the weaknesses in their plan,

- They learn a lot about themselves and their team, and

- They learn a lot about their market and how to go after it.

Finally, they really appreciate the respect shown to them for their time and the value they get.

Chapter 18

One Step At a Time: Overview of Deal Stages

Since I am part of a team that runs a very active angel network, most of the time, I am juggling a bunch of deals in different stages of completion. It can be hard to keep track of where everything stands. Obviously, regularly updated lists and status reviews are helpful, but even more helpful is an overall sense of each of the stages in the process. In particular it helps to know which stages are critical junctures and key turning points in the life of a deal. That way as deals make progress and are approaching those points, you can jump in proactively and help guide them along.

So what are these stages and how should a deal lead think about the overall process? As we have pointed out in our articles on diligence, we like to progress diligence in logical, sequential stages in order to conserve time and effort - that of the entrepreneur as well as the investors. It doesn't make sense to put a ton of work into an effort if you have no likelihood of investing. So a process designed with checkpoints along the way is the best approach.

A good basic process will include the following stages:

- Initial Pitch Meeting

- Deep Dive Meeting

- Due Diligence Phase & Goal Alignment

- Negotiation of Terms

- Solicitation of Soft-Circles

- Syndication

- First Closing

Let's have Christopher take us through a closer look at each of these stages at an overview level.

Q

Christopher, how do initial meetings work? Are you talking about screening, or a formal pitch

Pitching companies typically are introduced to the investors by a trusted source and then selected and invited to pitch as a result of making it through some form of screening process. Active early stage investors will look at anywhere from 50-100 companies for each company they actually invest in. Angels invest in a lot of companies, but say no to the significant majority of companies they speak with.

Screening is typically done by a committee or subset of the investors in a network. The companies which make it through screening will typically progress to a pitch in front of the full group or network. These pitches are almost always relatively short in duration - somewhere between 10 and 30 minutes, with a 15-20 slide deck as a guide, and some time for questions and answers after the presentation.

> We like to progress
> diligence in logical,
> sequential stages in
> order to conserve time
> and effort - that of the
> entrepreneur as well as
> the investors.

Well-crafted pitches will typically cover a pretty wide gamut of topics, including:

- Description of the Customer Problem

- Overview of the Product/Solution

- Team/Key Players

- Market Opportunity

- Competitive Landscape

- Go To Market Strategy

- Stage of Development & Key Milestones

- Critical Risks and Challenges

- Financial Model & Projections

- Funding Requirements & Use of Funds

- Exit/Liquidity Options

If the pitch and Q&A goes well, a presenting company will typically progress to a more lengthy session. Many groups including Launchpad refer to this next lengthy meeting as a "deep dive meeting."

Q

What do you mean by a "Deep Dive?" How do those meetings work? Who attends? Is there a formal agenda?

The deep dive meeting (see Appendix for example deep dive meeting notes) is pretty much exactly what it sounds like. A longer format meeting, typically two or more hours, to unpack the story in a little bit greater detail than can be done in a pitch. If a pitch is a quick check of investor interest, a deep dive is a chance to qualify that interest and see if there is enough substance to merit forming a due diligence team. Deep dive meetings typically involve the investors most interested in the company based on the initial pitch meeting. And, not surprisingly, the diligence team is recruited from these deep dive volunteers.

In most cases, there will be 2-5 themes or clusters of key questions that arise during the pitch. The deep dive is focused on these questions; the questions should be organized into an informal agenda with time allocations. To make the meeting most effective, the company should receive in advance an overview of the key topics to be covered and the key questions which were brought up at their presentation. And the meeting should be actively monitored to keep it on schedule and ensure that all the key topics are touched on.

As noted in an earlier question, a good diligence process progresses through a series of checkpoints.

- Screening is one,

- A successful pitch is another,

- And a deep dive is a big one.

Forming a team and undertaking a diligence process is a lot of work for investors, and a lot of time and distraction for founders. It should not be undertaken on a whim. Therefore many companies progress no further.

At Launchpad, slightly over 50% of the time, interest in the company diminishes after the deep dive and we halt discussions with the company. The decision need not be unanimous, but it must be crisp and clear. If the majority lacks interest, it is important to be definitive and not waste investor or company time.

Diligence causes some attrition and fatigue; it is a disaster to go in with too few volunteers and too little conviction. It is better for all involved to make a clean break and step out of the lead role. If the company finds another lead and gets the round going, investors can always peel off and circle back and join the round under another group's leadership. But a group with insufficient enthusiasm should not undertake the deal lead role. It is bad for everybody involved.

If interest remains after the deep dive meeting, we select a deal lead and launch into the next phase of due diligence.

> Goal alignment is about making sure everyone wants and expects the same things out of the company. Goal alignment is typically used to establish common ground around the long range plans of the company.

Q

When noting the section of diligence, you called the main phase "due diligence & goal alignment." Why do you give "goal alignment" the same billing as due diligence?

They get equal billing because diligence is really a combination of

micro and macro. You need the team to delve into the details of the business and build and test an investment hypothesis. But the deal lead's job is to simultaneously keep an eye on the big picture:

- Are the investors and founders on the same page?

- Is this a deal that is going to work?

Goal alignment is about making sure everyone wants and expects the same things out of the company. Goal alignment is typically used to establish common ground around the long range plans of the company. It's crucial to make sure the investors and the founders are in sync and want and expect the same things. Goal alignment needs to cover a variety of areas, including:

- Long term company objectives

- Use of funds and aggressiveness of investment levels

- Long range financing plans and assumptions

- Exit strategies and expectations on size and timing

One of the key conversations the deal lead should have with the CEO revolves around where and how fast the company is planning to spend the cash investors are supplying. This "Use of Funds" discussion presents an interesting test for the early working relationship because it involves some tricky questions. Key hot button topics that frequently come up include compensation for the management team, key initial hires and marketing spend.

It is also important to figure out if there is agreement on what we need to learn about product / market fit before we pour on the gas. Is there a consensus about how many new markets we will enter simultaneously?

Another set of alignment-oriented questions might be along the lines of:

• What are the growth milestones that allow the company to raise a future round of financing at a favorable valuation to the early investors?

• Will there be enough funding from this early round to allow the

company to achieve these important growth milestones?

As the diligence team is unearthing key details of the plan, the deal lead's role is to fit that information into the overall big picture puzzle and make sure there is alignment on goals.

Another very important by-product of the goal alignment process is laying a foundation for the long term relationship between the deal lead and the CEO. It is fairly typical for a deal lead to end up being a board member or at least a close advisor to the company or liaison to investors. Over a period of 6 to 8 weeks, the deal lead will spend a fair amount of time interacting with the CEO. This is an important time to establish the basis for a longer term working relationship. If possible, it helps to spend time getting to know the CEO on a more personal basis. The goal is to make sure you are comfortable working together for the next several years.

Q

Goal alignment sounds awfully close to a negotiation. When does the negotiation stage formally start? How do you know it is time? Who is in charge of it? How do the issues from diligence play into it?

It has been observed that everything is a negotiation, and that is probably true in this context. Every interaction tells you something about the management team and informs your approach to deal formation. Many of the issues uncovered by the diligence team will have implications for terms like valuation and size of round. And, you often discuss with the CEO, at least preliminarily, big issues like valuation range, size of round and board representation as a sanity check and condition of inviting a company in to pitch.

But all that said, the formal negotiation really should not start in earnest until it is virtually certain that the diligence team will reach a positive recommendation. It is true that you could shave a little time off if you started a bit earlier, but that can prove to be a disastrous mistake for a couple of reasons:

- If the team suddenly uncovers a "deal breaker" issue and decides the deal is uninvestable, you will have a mess on your hands trying to explain that to founders with whom you already started negotiating deal terms.

- If the team finds an issue, that is not important enough to kill the deal, but has big implications in terms of valuation, you are going to find it extremely hard to re-trade the price of the deal if you have already floated a higher number. It does not matter that you found a new issue - the entrepreneurs will always experience it like you are reneging on the deal.

So it is generally best to wait until the team has reached a positive consensus and begun drafting their diligence report. At that point you can begin to flesh out a termsheet.

There are two ways to go about forming a termsheet: you can walk the CEO through the concepts and your thoughts before showing it to them, or you can just send them a proposed draft termsheet. I generally base my approach on the sophistication level of the founding team. If they are very experienced and familiar with early stage investing terms, I will generally just prepare a draft termsheet and send it to them.

> Formal deal term negotiations really should not start in earnest until it is virtually certain that the diligence team will reach a positive recommendation.

But, if they are new to the whole investment process and some context and education and perspective might help them better understand the termsheet and react to it more constructively, then I will generally have a conversation and explain the various issues and where I am coming from on each point before sending it over. That way they know roughly what to expect and are not surprised by the harsh black and white of the terms on paper.

Q

What do you mean by soft-circle? What is going on and how does that process work? What is the role of the deal lead? Are there better and worse ways to do it?

A soft-circle is an indication of interest by an investor in a deal. It typically involves the investor specifying an actual dollar amount they are willing to invest in this round with this company. It is called "soft" because it is conditioned on the final terms being acceptable and as described in the termsheet.

Soft-circles are an essential tool for two reasons. First they allow a deal lead and entrepreneur to run around and line everyone up and rally support for the deal. The mounting cumulative total of the soft-circles is really the yardstick of the deal's progress and momentum. If they accumulate quickly, or at least steadily, it is an indication that the terms of the deal are going to be acceptable to the market.

Secondly, soft-circles are a way of holding investors and money in suspension while you line up one or two orchestrated closings. People are mentally committed to the deal, but they have not yet written a check. So they are on-board but held in suspension while you get the minimum money needed for the first close.

This ability to hold committed investors in suspension is invaluable because closings are a fair amount of work and involve coordination and transactional expense working with outside counsel. This is because the key terms of the deal are effectuated by means of a new class of preferred shares and these are memorialized by the filing of a revised certificate of incorporation in Delaware or another state of incorporation. Closings also involve the collection of a lot of signatures on a lot of documents as well as the transmission of a lot of checks. It is much more efficient to do all that work at once in one big organized orchestrated way than to have money trickling in over weeks and months.

Soft-circles can be solicited any number of ways; via email, telephone or a webform. At Launchpad we use a simple webform which results in a cloud spreadsheet (for example, Google Forms and Google Docs). This way, all the information is in one organized place and the resulting cloud spreadsheet can be shared with the entrepreneur and their attorney. In fact, we often let the entrepreneur use the webform for other investors who are not in our group. And, they can embellish the cloud spreadsheet with other notes and annotations that everyone involved in the deal administration can see. Since we are consistent in using Google Forms, the investors in Launchpad are familiar and comfortable with the process. We can easily post and circulate new investments to our investors. Very effective, yet fast, light and efficient.

Q

You've referred to a "first close." Are there others? Is this syndication? What is a syndication and how does it work? For that matter, why is it called syndication?

Yes, yes, it is all related. In finance, the term syndication refers to bringing groups or entities together into a transaction. In early stage investing it is about showing the deal to different investors, groups, networks, or funds to have them join the collection of investors funding the deal.

Often this kind of collaboration is necessary to fill the deal since each individual investor is only contributing a small amount relative to the overall round size. But regardless of whether it is necessary, it is often desirable since it builds a stronger, broader and more diversified financial base for the company to rely on in future rounds. And it gives the company a broader network of investors who can advise, help and make introductions.

The way syndication typically works is the lead investor and their network or closest associates will be in the first close. Once the closing minimum is met, the company has a close and can start putting the money to work. Then, the deal lead will accelerate the process of presenting the deal to other investors. Not only will they have a termsheet and diligence report, they will have two other key advantages:

- They now have some momentum to show - they can show that a good chunk of money has already closed, and additional soft circles are piling up.

- They have scarcity - the round is starting to fill up - a consensus is emerging and it is time to move or you will be left behind.

Momentum and scarcity are absolutely key ingredients for deal leads looking to get investors to move.

Q

What is a closing? Why are they necessary? How should a deal lead be involved with a closing?

As noted above, a closing is an orchestrated transaction involving the company and all the investors signing and exchanging deal documents, sending in money and making filings with the state and federal regulators. Because closings are a fair amount of work and involve coordination and transactional expense working with outside lawyers, you want to have as few closings as possible and have each one be as big as possible. This is because the key terms of the deal are effectuated by means of a new class of preferred shares and these are memorialized by the filing of a revised certificate of incorporation in Delaware or another state of incorporation.

Closings, in conjunction with closing minimums, allow for a very important protection for investors, who fear being the first person to invest and having their money stuck in an under-funded company. A closing with a defined minimum needed to close gives investors the certainty that their money will not be released to the company until a certain minimum viable dollar threshold has been met.

A deal lead's role in a closing is to keep the lines of communication open with investors on timing and expectations, and to advise the company on how not to screw it up. The way most companies screw it up is by sending the closing package from hell – the biggest "unforced error" in all of early stage investing.

Every investor has experienced it. A giant mess of documents arrives via email late on a Friday night from some person you never heard of. Some documents are in PDF, some Excel, the rest in MS Word. They are all dumped into the bottom of an unclear email demanding immediate attention and response. The documents are inscrutably named, with long strings of digits from internal file system numbers.

When investors start to wade in, nowhere is it made clear what documents they are supposed to sign and what documents are for information only. Nowhere does it indicate where in the document they are supposed to sign. Nor is it ever made clear that several documents need to be signed in two places and one in three. And of course some documents are only for existing investors whereas others need to be signed by everyone.

A deal lead can and should make sure everyone is clear on the closing process and it gets done on time as expected. They should keep on top of the company to communicate with investors to make sure the follow-ups happen:

- Counter-signed documents go out,

- Stock certificates (or receipts or electronic certificates) go out,

- A summary of the final close and company financing status goes out.

Chapter 19

Many Hands, Light Work: The Team Approach to Processing Deals

Do you remember the first time you became excited about investing in an early stage technology company? You were impressed by the CEO and you loved the market opportunity. But, you knew you had to dig deep to find out whether there was a real winner in the making. So, you took a step back and started putting together a list of all the questions you had and the research you needed to do before making an investment. It felt a bit like being back in college and working on a major research paper. You were excited by the project, but daunted by the amount of work!

Even when you right-size the process and try to focus on the major issues, diligence can be a lot of work. It can be fun, and if you are trying to build a diversified portfolio of 10 or more investments and do all your own diligence, you are going to burn out long before you are diversified. Plus, you probably won't do as good a job working on your own as you could if you had some help.

A team approach brings more hands, more eyes, more perspective and more expertise in areas where you may be less knowledgeable. Angel investors working together in groups address the biggest tension in early stage investing. This is the tension between the need to be diversified in this asset class to win, and the fact that, done right, each deal represents a lot of work. Properly constructed diligence teams are a perfect way to address this tension.

Q

Ham, you formed and led a lot of diligence teams in your 15+ year angel career. What resources are you working with when forming a team? What is the deal lead's role in putting the team together and making it work?

The very nature of a team means you are not working alone. Everyone on the team should have a well-defined job. As the deal lead, it is your responsibility to divide up and delegate tasks based on the diligence checklist you put together. Your team should have people with applicable skills and knowledge in the areas that you need to research. If you don't have the right skills internally, you might need to reach out into your group's external network to find appropriate skills. For example, at Launchpad, we work with our attorney to help us on the occasional Intellectual Property review.

> Angel investors working together in groups address the biggest tension in early stage investing. This is the tension between the need to be diversified in this asset class to win, and the fact that, done right, each deal represents a lot of work.

Once you have each of the key risk areas covered by one of your team members, the deal lead's role evolves. Now, you own the ultimate responsibility for making sure things move forward in a smooth, timely fashion. This includes:

- Gathering documents and important materials from the company,

- Making sure your team members are completing their assignments,

- Assembling the content and editing the final due diligence report,

- Keeping things on track and hitting your deadline for a final investment decision.

Needless to say, a great deal lead tends to be an individual who likes to manage teams and projects. If that doesn't fit your personal/work profile, you should probably reconsider whether you should be a deal lead.

What does it mean to be on a diligence team? What is a typical time commitment and set of expectations?

As a diligence team member, you will volunteer to take on a specific diligence assignment, such as customer reference checks or a competitive review. With a well defined task, your job is to assemble the appropriate information in a timely fashion.

During the diligence effort, the deal lead manages activities and requests with the entrepreneur to ensure professionalism and coordination. Each team member is expected to be responsive to other team members and timely with their deliverables.

Most diligence assignments are relatively specific and should be completed within a reasonable amount of time. Depending on the task, your work effort should fall within a range of 2 to 8 hours. For the entire diligence team, with everyone working in parallel, the typical diligence process can be completed in 20 to 40+ person hours of work. By working in parallel, a diligence team should be able to wrap up their assessment of the company and publish a report within a month.

Q

How do you approach the question of tools? Is there special due diligence software you are supposed to use? Is there one proper way to produce the work product?

There are many ways to approach the question of tools to support the due diligence process. At Launchpad, we apply tools to all of our processes with the philosophy that you want to be pretty heavy on the tools in the beginning at the deal flow stage with a deal flow management system, and pretty heavy at the post-investment stage with a good portfolio management system, but you want to keep it pretty light and loose in the middle during diligence. We therefore apply tools in the following manner:

- **Deal Flow** - We use a sophisticated content management system that helps us track our interactions with the hundreds of companies that apply to Launchpad every year. This system is well organized, supports a lot of different views into the data, and allows us to closely follow a company as it progresses from their initial application to our group all the way up to the due diligence stage.

- **Due Diligence** - We deliberately allow our deal leads and diligence participants to use a collection of comfortable off-the-shelf, simple products to help manage diligence. All of the products (see below), are tools that most business people are familiar with, having used many of them for work or personal activities.

- **Portfolio Management** - Once we invest in a company, we want to track that company as part of our overall portfolio. At Launchpad, and for our personal early stage portfolios, we use Seraf to stay on top of our investments, gain visibility, track performance, and report on our portfolio.

For the entire diligence team, with everyone working in parallel, the typical diligence process can be completed in 20 to 40+ person hours of work. By working in parallel, a diligence team should be able to wrap up their assessment of the company and publish a report within a month.

There are four types of tools that we make frequent use of during the due diligence process. All of these tools are free, web-based platforms. Some of these products have more full featured, paid subscriptions. So here's what we recommend you put in place:

- **Deal Room** - The Deal Lead should set up a shared folder in the cloud (e.g. DropBox but other cloud folders will work) and invite team members to the folder. Materials can be collected there for everyone's reference.

- **Meeting Scheduler** - Coordinating calendars for a group of individuals is never easy. You will need a meeting scheduler (e.g. Doodle, TimeBridge, NeedToMeet) to conduct scheduling polls to arrange meetings.

- **Conference Calls** - Most meetings during the diligence process will be handled by conference call. You will need a conference calling service for this reason (e.g. UberConference, FreeConferenceCall).

- **Diligence Report** - As we noted in our eBook on due diligence, the Deal Lead should consider assembling the report in Google Docs so that everyone can see each others' work as it comes together. See the Appendix for a diligence report template.

Chapter 20

Every Team Needs A Coach: Managing the Deal Process

Not everyone is cut out to lead a deal. In our experience, it takes a certain temperament and set of people skills to lead a bunch of peer volunteers. There are many successful investors who cringe at the phrase, "managing the process." Managing is the last thing they see themselves doing. The good news is that early stage investing seems to attract a lot of people who are motivated, take-charge people who are looking to help out and give back. So there are many early stage investors who love to "manage." Maybe they were product managers or some form of group leader in their career. Or, maybe they just love being organized and leading group efforts.

Ham spent a good part of his early career as a product manager for a software company. So he's one of those folks who is skilled at and enjoys managing a team process. In the early days at Launchpad, he pulled together the guidelines that evolved into the processes we use today in every one of our due diligence efforts.

> The first time you lead a deal, it can be a bit overwhelming. This is where strong organizational skills and an ability to work toward a goal come into play. Having a well-thought-out checklist and a well-coordinated team will make your job easier.

Q

Ham, assuming an individual is the type of person who enjoys managing a process, what does it actually take to "manage the process?"

It all comes down to the checklist. The first time you lead a deal, it can be a bit overwhelming. This is where strong organizational skills and an ability to work toward a goal come into play. Having a well-thought-out checklist and a well-coordinated team will make your job easier. A willingness and ability to delegate tasks across a good sized group of 6 to 12 individuals is crucial. Taking on many of the tasks by yourself is defeating the purpose... remember, diligence is a team sport!

Q

What are the main tasks the deal lead is really doing in their leadership role?

There are a handful of major responsibilities that a deal lead must be willing to buy into to ensure a successful diligence process. They include:

- **Keeping the process moving** - If diligence drags on, the likelihood of a successful deal diminishes rapidly. You don't want speed for speed's sake, but you do need to push the team to complete all the assigned tasks.

- **Communicating with the team on a regular basis** - Without regular communications, it's very common for diligence team members to slack off on their assignments. By communicating with the team on a weekly basis, you are applying subtle pressure to get all assignments completed.

- **Coordinating interactions with the company** - Just as diligence team members need to be in the loop, so does the company CEO. You want to make sure they know what's going on with your team. And, you will help coordinate any meetings your team might need with members of company management.

- **Maintaining a positive and supportive (but objective) tone** - It's easy to find all the "warts" with an early stage company. Helping your team members (especially the less optimistic ones) maintain a reasonable perspective on what an early stage company should and shouldn't be able to achieve in its first years is critical. That said, you are not a cheerleader for the company. So make sure you maintain a proper balance when working with your team.

- **Creating a succinct but thorough and professional diligence report** - Are you going to read a 40 page diligence report filled with lots and lots of details? I doubt it! So why would you want to write a 40 page report? Through lots of trial and error, and after reading a few 40 page reports produced by other investors, we came up with a succinct format for diligence reports. So, keep it short, thorough and professional, even if that means editing one of your team member's 5 page "summary" on their assignment down to 2 or 3 paragraphs.

Q

What are some traps for the unwary?

I can think of dozens of ways that the diligence process runs into real problems. Over the years, we've run into many situations that made us rethink how to best run our diligence teams. And, we've heard war stories from other early stage investors that helped to shape our approach to diligence. I won't write an exhaustive list of traps, but here's a list of some of the most common problems:

- **Too much 1:1 communication** - As a deal lead, there will be times when you need to have a quick conversation with a team member. That's okay as long as it's not your standard operating procedure. You are better off having a weekly conference call to make sure that your entire team is in sync. And, it's a more efficient use of your time, as well.

- **Too many long conference calls** - This trap is pretty obvious. Your team members will become bored and burned out. Stick with, at most, a weekly call and make sure

it lasts less than 1 hour… and shorter than that is even better.

- **Trying to force a consensus too early** - Just because you are 100% positive on the company and are ready to write a check doesn't mean that other team members are too. It's best to let individual team members pull together their summaries and then move towards a consensus.

- **Arguing with findings and having a bias** - It's very rare for all findings during diligence to trend positive. And, there is nothing wrong with discovering some negative issues. In my personal view, any diligence report that doesn't have any negatives is a bit suspect. Accept what your team uncovers, so that your final report is fair and balanced.

- **Allowing team members to let the team down** - You have to stay on top of each team member and make sure they complete their assignments in a timely fashion. Hopefully, you won't end up with any foot draggers, but there are times when life gets in the way. Whether it be vacation, work or personal issues, there will be team members who can't complete their assignment. It's your job to replace that team member so the overall process completes on time.

- **Not resolving personality conflicts** - Sometimes people will get lumped together on a sub-team and they just don't gel and cannot seem to work together. You need to be alert to these kinds of frictions and fix them before they impact deliverable quality or timeliness, or undermine team morale. You also don't want to have the entrepreneur see investors fighting. Your job is to get in there and swap someone out for a replacement before frictions escalate.

No matter the context, every leader has to motivate his/her team, has to be clear about expectations, has to be organized, and has to be diligent. So keep that in mind as you develop your style of team leadership.

Q

Should you be looking for one particular style of leadership? Does a deal lead have to be a type A drill sergeant barking orders to be effective?

Over the years at Launchpad, we've worked with more than two dozen different deal leads. As you would expect, deal leadership styles differ. So, feel free to adapt our recommendations on process so it works for you. That said, some of the basic guidelines related to communications and coordination are critical. No matter the context, every leader has to motivate his/her team, has to be clear about expectations, has to be organized, and has to be diligent. So keep that in mind as you develop your style of team leadership.

Q

How about a situation where diligence leadership can go off the rails?

One of the biggest challenges in doing diligence reviews is knowing when to stop and when to press ahead. As we noted in our eBook on Due Diligence, the diligence process is a fickle beast - there are times when it takes discipline to keep going in the face of mounting issues, and there are times when it takes discipline to call a time-out despite accelerating deal momentum.

It can be very discouraging to get into a diligence project and begin finding issues and realizing the story is not as complete and attractive as you first thought it was. The desire to quit the effort can be very seductive. Equally seductive is the desire to minimize or ignore late-breaking issues once you've already put a ton of time and work into a deal. In both cases, allowing yourself to be seduced in the moment can lead to big mistakes.

> You need a framework that builds in natural evaluation points or circuit breakers to give you the opportunity to reestablish your perspective and honestly review where you are relative to where you think you should be.

The deal lead's role is crucial in this regard. Diligence is not only about identifying risks, it is about putting those risks in perspective and figuring out which ones matter and which ones don't. You need a framework that builds in natural evaluation points or circuit breakers to give you the opportunity to reestablish your perspective and honestly review where you are relative to where you think you should be. And you need a deal lead who's not mired in all the detail work but can step back and see the big picture.

Chapter 21

"Places, Please!"
Organizing A Deal Team

Even with a right-sized approach, every time I get into a project, I am always reminded that diligence is still a fair amount of work. At Launchpad we estimate that we spend around 40 person hours on a typical diligence process by the time the project is completed. If you are dealing with busy investors who are volunteering to do this work, burnout is a real risk.

6 Ways to Manage a Deal Team

Given the number of deals we do in a year and the pace at which we move, we cannot afford burnout. So we work to manage it in six ways:

- We utilize a larger overall team size consisting of a dozen or more people organized in small sub-teams working in parallel;

- We base involvement on an opt-in approach where people self-select and volunteer as their passions dictate;

- We don't move forward unless there is spontaneous enthusiasm and interest from enough volunteers;

- We let people choose their area of focus so they can be in their area of expertise and comfort zone;

- We augment teams by tapping uninvolved investors for discrete questions and input on specialty topics; and

- We are clear about the process and the deliverables so that people don't waste effort and do more work than is absolutely necessary.

Still, it is a lot of work. We begin the pre-diligence process (i.e. deep dive meeting) on 20-25 companies a year, and push through to final due diligence reports on 8-12 companies a year. So it helps in our case that we have a large pool of 150 investors to recruit from. We can arrange it so our investors do not have to participate in diligence more than once every 12-18 months unless they want to.

Christopher organizes most of our diligence teams, so let's ask him how this works and what advice he has on the process.

Q

Christopher, where do you start when forming a team?

The team forms in a couple stages. Overall, our process is to start wide, and end wide, but be more narrow in the middle. By that I mean:

- All our investors see the company pitch,

- All see the final diligence report and get a chance to soft-circle invest,

- But, a smaller number are involved in the diligence sausage-making in the middle.

Here is how we do it:

During a pitch we ask all investors to indicate their interest level. Indicated levels can range from "not interested" to "would consider investing" to the highest level of interest, "willing to help with diligence." We also ask people to let us know if they have particular resources or connections that might be helpful to a company.

Once we have those investor indications of interest, we do some number crunching. We look at:

- Total absolute interest levels

- Relative interest levels on a percentage-of-attendees basis

- Skill level of those interested (because if all our experts on the subject hate it, but the uninformed love it, that can be a problem)

If you cannot get your experts to engage with a deal, that is a big red flag. It is tantamount to having the people who know most about the subject like the deal the least. That is pretty telling. In those situations, it is best to set the opportunity aside and move on to something else.

Based on these three indicators, we figure out which companies have enough critical mass to merit a deep dive meeting. At one of our monthly group meetings, it can range from none to all three of the presenting companies making the cut, but typically two out of the three presenting companies will earn a deep dive.

From there we get some possible deep dive dates from the company and then put it out to all the investors expressing interest in the form of a deep dive scheduling poll. And then we do some number crunching again to find the deep dive date that is going to have the largest and strongest team we can field. Typically, that results in a deep dive meeting of anywhere from 10 to 25 investors, with 15 to 20 being the normal attendance range.

> Angel investors are often very connected people who are good at bridging to other connected people. Be sure to tap into the power of that network.

Before the deep dive meeting ends, we ask the CEO and her team to give us the room and we take the temperature of the investors.

- If no one really likes the company, we are done.

- If a few people like it, but not enough to form a team and no one wants to step up as a deal lead, then we are done.

- If a plurality like it and want to form a team, and we can find someone to volunteer as a deal lead, then we take down all the names and the deal lead is off to the races on forming the team, assigning the roles and laying out the project plan.

Q

How do you document the assignments?

Regardless of outcome, we always send out deep dive notes which capture the deep dive discussion in a Q&A format, and also capture the next steps. If the next steps are that we are not moving forward, we note that. If we are moving forward, we note who the lead will be and sketch out the volunteers, sometimes even noting who is going to cover which topic areas. We email that information out with a note that volunteers should stand by for

168

further communication from the deal lead. Then, off-line, we coordinate with the deal lead on getting a team organized, building a project plan and getting a "next steps" email out to everyone.

Q

What if you don't have enough expertise in the room? What do you do? Do you ever hire experts?

Venture capitalists will sometimes hire outside experts to help with their diligence, but angels and smaller funds generally cannot afford to do that. They must rely on their own expertise and connections to evaluate deals. Fortunately, investors tend to like and be drawn toward companies in their area of expertise, so your best experts for any given company tend to show up and volunteer. And, we pay a lot of attention to the topography of skills in our group and try to focus our deal flow and pitching companies exclusively in areas where we have competence.

Sometimes, for one reason or another, you won't have all your experts in the room at a deep dive. So you need to go out and manually recruit your experts to help fill out the gaps with the team. If you cannot get your experts to engage with a deal, that is a big red flag. It is tantamount to having the people who know most about the subject like the deal the least. That is pretty telling. In those situations, it is best to set the opportunity aside and move on to something else. Investing in areas where you have no expertise on the diligence team is a fool's errand. It is initially a waste of valuable human capital, and then later, invariably proves to be a waste of valuable financial capital.

If your team's inherent expertise is not sufficient, you may not need to give up or hire experts. If you can get the word out to people that you are looking for subject matter expertise in a certain area, you will be surprised at what you can find with a little networking. Angel investors are often very connected people who are good at bridging to other connected people. Be sure to tap into the power of that network.

And don't forget significant others - we once found much needed expertise in the spouse of an investor.

personal style of working and make sure they have the tools and info they need to be successful, as well as offer a good experience to their fellow investors.

Q

Once you have a deal lead and team, what do you do next?

Our group manager works with the deal lead to:

- Familiarize him/her with all the tools and checklists available,

- Look at the calendar to put an overall plan together,

- Set dates for key items like interim status calls and first draft of report,

- Help get workspaces like shared folders set up, and

- Work on the next steps/call to action email to the team.

How involved that collaboration is depends a lot on the experience level of the deal lead. If they have done it many times before, it is pretty hands off. Either way we are looking to respect their own

> It all gets easier with a little practice. Most new deal leads tell me they enjoyed leading a deal much more the second time through.

Q

Sounds basic, what's so hard about this?

The basics are easy. Doing it well takes a little practice. The goal is to use both investor and entrepreneur time efficiently. You want to avoid confusion, duplication of effort, and diffusion of responsibility. You want everybody to own something and

170

everything to be owned by someone.

There are lots of little tricky spots to trip you up; for example, you need to make sure you:

- Confirm team members and topic leaders so that you don't find out two weeks into the project that no one is working on competition or the financial plan,

- Have collected all the sub-teams' information requests so that you can hit the company with one consolidated request rather than have every sub-team chasing them separately,

- Know about vacations of key players on your team and at the company,

- Don't accidentally invite the company to the investors' data room,

- Don't copy the company on key investor communications, and

- Keep calm and keep your perspective throughout the process.

It all gets easier with a little practice. Most new deal leads tell me they enjoyed leading a deal much more the second time through. And the most fun of all is when an experienced deal lead ends up on a deal with a great team, where everything comes together well and ends up in an enthusiastically positive outcome.

Chapter 22

Grist For The Mill: Gathering Data for Diligence

Do you know what the magic moment is when an entrepreneur can say to her team that she is in diligence with a potential investor? It's certainly not at the first meeting with the investor. And, most likely it's not at the second meeting. At Launchpad, we take care to be clear about when a company is in diligence and when they are not. The reason for this is twofold.

First, there is the signaling risk - we take a good number of companies to the deep dive stage, but only about half of them into diligence. If a company in the deep dive stage is running around town saying they are in diligence with us, they run about a 50% chance of giving themselves a black eye and having to explain why our "diligence" came out negative.

Second, we don't want frustrated expectations or surprises that can leave a company pissed off and feeling misled. If they are in a situation where they have about a 50% chance of moving forward, we want them to understand that so that they have the right perspective.

So we go out of our way to make the probabilities as clear as we can by sharing historical averages and making our process as transparent as possible. Overall our ratios look something like this:

- less than 50% of the companies reaching out will be scouted,

- less than 50% of the companies scouted will come out positively,

- about 1/3 of the companies with positive scouting reports are invited to pitch,

- about 2 out of 3 pitching companies earn a deep dive,

- about 50% of the companies earning a deep dive make it into and through diligence to investment.

In practice, this translates into something in the neighborhood of a 3-5% hit rate. So it pays to be clear with the company about where they stand. Only if all goes well at the deep dive, can the entrepreneur report back to her team that she is in diligence with Launchpad. Most early stage investment organizations have a slight variation on this process, but it is pretty typical that it will take 2 to 4 meetings with the entrepreneur before investors are ready to do the heavy-lifting involved with diligence.

> The trick to doing diligence well, and to keeping the process speedy and efficient, is coordination. By that, I mean coordination of requests and coordination in storage. If your goal is a professional and efficient experience for both CEOs and investors, you don't want a chaotic process where everyone is playing off a different sheet of music.

Diligence focuses on discovering and understanding the key risks in a company. This is achieved by asking lots of questions and reviewing many documents. If diligence is fundamentally the review and evaluation of information, it stands to reason that the information needs to be collected first. Some bits of information will always be trickling in throughout the process, but most projects start with an initial information request for a big batch of the basics.

The trick to doing that well, and to keeping the process speedy and efficient, is coordination. By that, I mean coordination of requests and coordination in storage. If your goal is a professional and efficient experience for both CEOs and investors, you don't want a chaotic process where everyone is playing off a different sheet of music.

Let's get Ham's insights on how to orchestrate this.

Q

Ham, you've said that it all begins with the initial information request. What do you mean by that?

When pulling together an initial information request, you want to ask each member of the due diligence team to provide you with his/her list of required information before you do anything. That way you can engage the team members in the process and make sure they are thinking through their project. And, you want to avoid having each member hassle the CEO individually for this information. That's not a good experience for the CEO, nor is it calculated to get everything you need. So one consolidated initial information request is key. For a list of the types of information we typically ask for, the column titled "Information Request" in this due diligence checklist provides a great starting point.

Q

What do you do with all that information?

Everyone needs access to it. First, start by setting up two shared folders using Dropbox, Google Drive or some other tool that allows you to create a shared cloud folder to serve as a data room. The first shared folder will provide access to both the company and to all members of the diligence team. This allows the company to deposit documents, and all of the diligence team members to review the documents. Remember, some information is useful to more than one individual. The company should deposit all documents requested by your team in this folder.

A second shared folder should be set up for investor notes, draft reports, interview notes, etc. This allows all the investors on the team to see each other's progress. This folder is visible only to the diligence team. The company does not have access. It pays to be careful about permissions and carefully labeling links when you share these folders - a pro tip is to name them descriptively, for example "Investor Only NewCo DD Folder."

Q

Why is it so important to have a private investor-only folder? Wouldn't it be helpful to get the company's feedback on key issues?

Well, you definitely want, and should get, the company's take on major issues that crop up, but if you let the company read your report and notes and involve them in your report creation process, three things happen:

1. You are not writing the investor's story, you are rehashing the company's take on things. Diligence reports are supposed to be of investors, by investors and for investors.

2. You are going to chill the honesty of the team members, and that is not a good thing. You want candor and straight talk. If they know the company is going to read what they write, they are going to worry about ruffled feathers and their reputation, etc.

3. The CEO is going to get distracted and bent out of shape over all sorts of little things. Early stage diligence does not turn on little things. With early stage diligence, the point is to get the overall big picture right. The exact assumptions going into each model are not critical, it is the overall conclusion that matters, and it is usually right, even if one small detail is off.

Q

Once the information requests are out, what comes next?

The team members are going to need to speak to the company, so the deal lead's role is to facilitate those meetings in an orderly fashion or at least provide some oversight to see that they are set up in an orderly fashion. For new entrepreneurs, it can be very overwhelming and nerve-wracking to have a bunch of investors swarm all over them about a bunch of different topics, so there is a role for the deal lead to coach them through the process.

Sometimes with larger, more built-out company teams, it works best to let individual diligence sub-teams meet with different people in the company separately. For example, the team building the financial model can meet with the person at the company who created this model. Or, the customer/go-to-market team can meet with the founders most responsible for sales

.

> Professionalism and respect matter. They should be a hallmark of all interactions. Don't be too skeptical, scornful, or disrespectful. It's important to been seen by the entrepreneur and her team as adding value in all exchanges.

Other times, when the company is just a small team of 2 to 4 individuals and all the diligence sub-

teams want to speak to the same couple of folks, it can make sense to build a stack of meetings where the founders meet with different sub-teams sequentially across a day or half day. That way it is efficient and different sub-teams can sit in on each other's meetings if they want to.

Q

What about subsequent follow up meetings?

Once a little bit of relationship and rapport is built up, it's ok for sub-teams to coordinate directly with the company to set up follow-on meetings or calls. The deal lead's job is to make sure one of those teams is not spinning its wheels and taking up tons of founder time obsessing about an issue for which there is not a good answer. Some investors, particularly new and inexperienced ones, get confused and think it is the company's job to explain all the risk away, and they can get frustrated or even combative and badger the company about why they don't know something. The deal lead's role is to keep an eye out for such inappropriate behavior and remind the investor that this is early stage investing and some things are best guesses. That's why valuations are low and the potential for return is high!

Even where there is no frustration, professionalism and respect matter. They should be a hallmark of all interactions. Don't be too skeptical, scornful, or disrespectful. It's important to been seen by the entrepreneur and her team as adding value in all exchanges. Diligence team members are effectively brand ambassadors for your organization. Remember, reasonable people can differ on many aspects of building an early stage company and there often is not one single right answer. Helping a CEO discover key risks and giving guidance on ways to address those risks go a long way to building your value in the eyes of the entrepreneurial community.

There is nothing worse than trying to run a good process and then finding out that the CEO is really upset because one bad apple on your team misbehaved and made everyone in your organization look bad. As deal lead, you have to stay on top of what's going on. Make sure you are cc'ed on all the emails (no matter how painful an impact on our inbox - remember it is temporary!) to make sure nothing is getting out of hand. You have to manage the quality of the entire process end-to-end, especially with diligence teams containing new investors who have not done it before or whom you don't yet know and trust.

Chapter 23

Forks In The Road: The Importance of Interim Checkpoints

If the business precept is true, that you "manage what you measure", checking in on your team with regular checkpoints is key to a successful process. Over the years we have run into a series of surprises with diligence teams. Sometimes we discover diligence teams that turned out to be off drilling dozens of dry wells. Other times we have CEOs call on a Sunday afternoon very distressed about an interaction with a member of the diligence team. From these surprises we learned that you really need to stay on top of things since they can go haywire fast. Similarly, diligence can go nowhere fast. It is all too frequent a situation where you think a sub-team is working on something and on schedule with it only to find out they have not done anything yet. You manage what you measure...

One of the biggest challenges in doing diligence reviews is knowing when to stop and when to press ahead. There are times when it takes discipline to keep going in the face of mounting issues, and there are times when it takes discipline to call a time-out despite accelerating deal momentum.

It can be very discouraging to get into a diligence project and begin finding issues and realizing the story is not as complete and attractive as you first thought it was. The desire to quit the effort can be very seductive. Equally seductive is the desire to minimize late-breaking issues once you have put a ton of time and work into a deal. In both cases, allowing yourself to be seduced in the moment can lead to big mistakes. So you need a framework that builds in natural evaluation points or circuit breakers to give you the opportunity to reestablish your perspective and honestly review where you are relative to where you think you should be.

The interim status call is just such a circuit-breaker. It forces people to collect their thoughts and assess where they are in a boiled-down fashion. It also keeps people moving. There is nothing like an approaching deadline for a public accounting of your progress to focus someone on a volunteer side project.

> One of the biggest challenges in doing diligence reviews is knowing when to stop and when to press ahead. There are times when it takes discipline to keep going in the face of mounting issues, and there are times when it takes discipline to call a time-out despite accelerating deal momentum.

Christopher has been overseeing dozens of these calls each year for many years, so let's get some insights into how to make them work.

Q

Christopher, when is the best time to have the first interim status call?

Diligence is all about momentum and getting things done before fatigue, boredom and other distractions overtake the project, so you want to have the first call as soon as you reasonably can. But there is little point in doing a call until people have had some time to do some work. So, assuming the company is responsive with information requests, I tend to aim for the end of the second week, or early in the third week. Regardless of when you actually place it, you need to publicize it ahead of time. The key is to put the call in the schedule early so people know it is coming and can self-manage to the deadline.

Q

How is the call facilitated?

You've nominated a deal lead for a reason, so it is best to let him/her lead the call. If the diligence team and deal lead are part of an angel network with professional management, there is plenty of time for the group manager to speak up during the discussion, but the manager shouldn't undermine its deal lead by monopolizing the call. A good manager will empower its deal lead by prepping together ahead of time and discussing goals and likely outcomes. But let the deal lead lead the call.

Q

How long should the call be, and what are you trying to cover?

No one likes long conference calls, so every effort should be made to keep it to an hour. You have a lot of sub-teams to hear from, and they have to cover a lot of factual findings, and then you need time for some synthesis. So it takes active facilitating to keep the call to an hour. That is an important part of the prep.

A format that works well is to start by having the different sub-teams summarize their findings so far. Note they should be summarizing their findings, **not** their activities. Everybody knows they worked hard and did a lot. What people need to hear about is if they found anything of note.

Once all the sub-teams have a chance to summarize their findings, if there are things that are just not baked yet, they become priorities for further work. This will result in follow up calls for the relevant sub-teams, and the deal lead should make sure those teams have an action plan and a due date.

Q

What do you do if you find a major yellow flag or diligence concern?

First of all, the deal lead should take the temperature of the group and see how people feel about the issue. Some items like entrepreneur integrity are going to be an absolute "game over" issue. Other items, like a serious competitor or a much less robust product than anticipated, are going to be a judgement call. So it is valuable for the deal lead to gather other people's reactions and not jump to their own conclusion. If it is not a show-stopper, then the focus should be on what additional work needs to be done in order to gauge the impact of this and put it into the proper perspective in the diligence report. If it is something that would likely stop the average investor from investing, then it is probably time to blow the whistle.

Q

If everything is going well, what is the next step?

Invariably one of the sub-teams is behind schedule or not done with their work or not available. Even in positive situations, there is more work to do before starting to draft the diligence report sections. Some sub-teams may be close to ready, so you can get the process started for them.

With the other teams it is more about agreeing on what steps they will take, what information they will gather, and what questions they will answer. The important part is to keep the team focused on the looming deliverable - their report section. This is not only key to getting reports done on time, it is key to making the process feel concrete and manageable to the participants. You can have the sub-teams that are in good shape take a first cut at their report section and invite them to share a draft with you for comment. With the sub-teams still contending with information gaps, you can talk to them about what specific information or analysis they think they will need before they can begin tackling their section.

> The important part is to keep the team focused on the looming deliverable - their report section. This is not only key to getting reports done on time, it is key to making the process feel concrete and manageable to the participants.

So it sounds like you may be starting the report drafting process at this point? How do you kick this off?

We are big believers in a very structured report template and all of our investors are familiar with it. So the teams mostly know what they are trying to accomplish with their section. There are three ways a deal lead can tackle report-building:

- Email everyone a copy of the template and say "fill out your section." Then the deal lead manually assembles it him or herself.

- Put the template on Google Docs, share the link and tell people to log in and fill in their section.

- Ask people to write unstructured memos on their findings and conclusions in their area. Then the deal lead assembles the final report.

There are pros and cons with each approach. Emailing a word document of the template is familiar and easy for everyone, but it can lead to a version control mess and a lot of email searching to find the right draft ("no, you used the one I sent at 10:10am on Tuesday, but I sent a later one in the same thread at 2:15pm. You should have used that one!").

Allowing everyone to create their own free form mini-memo shares the same familiarity and also the same version control issues. It also introduces the new problem of verbosity. The deal lead is going to have a ton of work editing a five page memo down to three paragraphs without changing the meaning or emphasis. The only good thing I can say about that approach is that sometimes the longer memo is nice to have in the supplemental files for investors who want to go deeper into a subject than the summary diligence report. The reality is that many "authors" have trouble going straight from a mass of unstructured notes and facts right to a tight couple of paragraphs, and will need the interim memo stage to help them organize their thoughts. So I don't discourage the practice, I just insist that they are not "done" when they give me a three page memo. **They also have to give me the three paragraph version.**

In my experience, sharing a Google Docs version of the template that can serve as a shared workspace and canonical version of the report is really the most efficient way to go about it. People can see each other's work and be guided and spurred on by the progress others are making, and they can be guided by the template. The deal lead can see exactly where each sub-team is at all times. And, the deal lead never has to be the version control manager or editor or file wrangler. They can say, "I've looked at your draft section, and I made some edits in redline" or "I like what you have but I need you to make it much shorter."

The only disadvantage with Google Docs is that some people are not as familiar with the tool and may have issues with losing their password, not finding a menu or command, or pasting their text into the document in gigantic purple letters (grin). And there is also the possibility that someone could put their elbow on their keyboard, select a lot of text and then delete a chunk of someone else's work. Google Docs does have version control so it is possible to roll-back in case that happens. Work will likely be lost if more than one person happens to be working right at the same time and you need to roll back to an earlier version. It's a rare issue, and worth the risk in my view. Plus, it can be mitigated by the proactive downloading and saving of copies by the deal lead or individual authors during the most active report writing times. We advise our deal leads to leave the document open in a browser tab and and download archival copies pretty regularly just for peace of mind.

You need to be careful not to get ahead of the final conclusion of the team. You need to be really sure you are done and coming out with a "go forward" recommendation. In a surprising number of cases, even when things start out looking positive, late-breaking issues can crop up and derail a diligence effort.

Q

If it is trending positive, do you communicate that to the company at this point?

The deal lead and the group manager should talk about that and approach it with caution. As we outlined in the Chapter 7, you need to be careful not to get ahead of the final conclusion of the team. You need to be really sure you are done and coming out with a "go forward" recommendation. In a surprising number of cases, even when things start out looking positive, late-breaking issues can crop up and derail a diligence effort. This is especially true of blind reference checks and customer calls which tend to happen later in the process.

So it is important to be very careful in talking to the company and to potential members of the syndicate too early. The company in particular will be listening for what they want to hear and it is very easy to get into a sticky situation where you have to surprise a team with new information that contradicts previous information.

That said, at some point, usually after a second check-in call or when most of the due diligence sections exist in draft form and things look good enough, it makes sense to start talking to the company about the termsheet negotiation and setting a deadline for completion of the project.

Chapter 24

Trust But Verify: The Importance of Reference Checking

There is an old Russian proverb that was adopted by Ronald Reagan during the later part of the Cold War and which became a signature phrase of Reagan's in the mid-1980s. When talking about the Russians, Reagan always liked to say we should "Trust, but Verify." It came to summarize the approach the US would use after the signing of a landmark nuclear disarmament treaty with the Russians.

At Launchpad, we like to follow this advice when it becomes clear that we like what we are hearing, and we believe there is solid investment opportunity with the company. That is the turning point where we start making reference calls on the management team and check in with customers. These conversations are critically important, but they tend to occur during the second half of the diligence process and for good reason.

Ham has gotten pretty good at these reference checks over the years, so let's figure out his tricks.

Q

Ham, first of all, if these reference checks are so important, why aren't you doing them sooner?

There are many reasons for delaying the start of "Trust, but Verify". An obvious reason is that it takes a fair amount of time, but that's much less important than the following reasons:

1. You don't want to bother your network and invade someone's privacy until you are reasonably sure you are going forward.

2. You do not want to disturb delicate existing customer relationships with intrusive investor questions unless you are pretty sure you are going forward. Interviews that remind customers of the shaky finances of their vendor are not ideal. That said, interviews with prospective customers with whom the company has no relationship are much less problematic.

3. All companies will provide you with a set of references that you should assume will have a positive bias. Other contacts should be "blind" reference checks with people in your network that know the CEO or other members of the management team. It takes time to work your network, so you often don't have good leads on blind references right away.

> You do not want to disturb delicate existing customer relationships with intrusive investor questions unless you are pretty sure you are going forward.

Q

How do you go about these management and customer reference checks?

During a typical due diligence process we run four different types of reference checks:

- Company-provided personal references

- Company-provided customer references

- Blind personal references

- Blind potential customer references

To keep the effort at a manageable level, we suggest you make two or three calls for each of these reference types. So, you are talking about eight to twelve calls that should last around 15-30 minutes each.

The deal lead should divide call assignments amongst the diligence team members. Personally, I like to give all the CEO reference checks to one person, all the management team checks to another, and then split the customer reference checks across one or two individuals. How you divide things up will be based on the size of your due diligence team.

At Launchpad, we have a well-defined set of questions we use to guide the management assessment interviews (see the appendix for our questionnaire.) It helps us uncover red flag issues that we need to keep an eye out for, and it helps us apply resources to help the CEO be successful. In addition, we have another set of questions that we use to guide our customer reference checks (see the appendix for our questionnaire.) And, if you use these two guides, you will have a consistent style of call notes that will help you when writing the summary diligence report.

You should initiate scheduling as soon as feasible, since these calls take time to set up. However, it is best to defer customer calls, in particular, until late in the process when positive outcome seems likely. That way, you don't disturb customers unless necessary. And, remember, back channel corroboration and blind reference checks via your organization's network are always VERY helpful.

Q

Besides reference checks, what else is going on at this stage in the process? Some groups are starting to draft their sections, but are others are still working?

Yes, there are always areas that require additional research. It takes time to recognize that need and time to find the resources and do the digging. In many cases, the company is still doing research to help you verify where the key risks lie, or responding to some of the

documents you asked for based on your diligence checklist. For example, they might be working on verifying the size of the market opportunity. And, you are also likely getting down into the details of the financial model at this point.

Your status calls will continue during this stage. It's always helpful for the team to hear how the references are trending. The deal lead should continue to update the CEO, as well (using some caution and circumspection, as noted above). Finally, based on how you are doing in completing the diligence checklist for this investment, the deal lead might need to assign one or two small research projects and enlist help, if needed, to fill information gaps and resolve important issues.

Chapter 25

Short and To the Point: Producing a Tight Report

We've all experienced pedantic people try to make their points by browbeating the listener. And we've all been frustrated by repetitive or long-winded people who just cannot get to the point. We just tune them out. They are not effective, whether in person or in writing. Diligence reports are the same - they won't help anyone if they go unread. And they will not be read if they are long and cumbersome. The extra length not only takes more time to wade through, it obscures key take-aways and impedes understanding. Producing a shorter report requires a bit more work and a bit more discipline, but it really makes for a better result. A short report can be supplemented with appendices, if needed, for that small subset of people who want more detail on a particular subject.

Experience has taught us that there are a few keys to getting a good short report done on time:

- Using a structured report template
- Making expectations clear
- Repeatedly stressing brevity
- Starting early and leaving time for revision
- Having a deal lead understand their role as an editor
- Seeking rewrites and revisions

As an English major with a law degree and experience with corporate communications, Christopher brings just the right skill set to help deal leads whip these reports into shape. Let's see what insights we can glean.

Q

Christopher, a lot of people really don't enjoy writing and tend to procrastinate when faced with a writing task. How do you get a group of investors to produce a tight report on time?

Focus on the deliverable. From the very beginning, before a Launchpad investor has even joined the network, we describe an individual's involvement in diligence as "doing a bit of research and producing a couple of paragraphs." Stress the deliverable throughout the process.

Q

But people are still going to procrastinate, aren't they?

Yes, with volunteer efforts, some slippage and procrastination is inevitable. No one is going to be pulling all-nighters to get their diligence report section done. But, it can be minimized with the careful application of a little peer pressure. If an organization has a culture of not letting colleagues down, as ours does, people will generally step up and be professional. Especially if you set clear expectations that it will get done. As noted in Chapter 8, that can be part of the value of creating the report in a shared workspace like Google Docs. People can see who is producing and who isn't. End of day, the report will be as late as its latest section, so calling each co-author and asking them if they have everything they need will make a big difference.

> If an organization has a culture of not letting colleagues down, as ours does, people will generally step up and be professional.

Q

When is the right time to get people writing? Is diligence ever done?

Diligence is never done, but it does approach a point of diminishing marginal returns pretty quickly. At some point additional work is not going to bring new insights or further de-risk the investment. These companies are early stage, so, for example, until they try their proposed go-to-market strategy and

see if it works, you just cannot know. So you have to have some tolerance for ambiguity and press ahead in the face of uncertainty.

And there can be real value in just putting pen to paper. As we all know from writing difficult correspondences, sometimes you don't really know what you are thinking or feeling until you actually sit down and begin to write the letter. Diligence is like that. Get people drafting early so they can figure out where their thoughts are and whether they have gaps that will require additional research. If everyone leaves it to the last minute, you will have a patchwork quilt full of holes.

Q

How much editing is required? Does the deal lead do it all?

The deal lead is responsible for overall production of the report, but I usually work with the deal leads to help with the editing. The goal is not to substitute your judgement for that of the team member, it is to stress brevity, force clarity, ensure consistency of quality, and eliminate basic typos and formatting mistakes. You want it in the words of the team members, but a little polish and clean up usually works wonders in terms of making it professional. Ninety percent of the editing we do is to push authors to make it shorter and boil it down to the bottom line.

Q

Do you recommend online collaboration on drafts or having teams email pieces of the report in for the deal lead to assemble?

Collaboration has a lot of advantages in that it allows people to see each other's work, and it forces people directly into the constraints of the template. You can make it work with people emailing sections, but you invariably get more words than you want. Then you have to assemble and boil down and edit yourself. And, then you need to recirculate to make sure that you have not paraphrased it incorrectly. Try as hard as you can to push people to give you their deliverable

in the final form you need. Transforming it yourself is a thankless task.

Q

Does every team member have a section to write?

Not necessarily. Most sub-teams will have more than one member, and a sub-team lead will do the initial drafting and circulate it for comments to other sub-team members. This is essential when a team is divided. Our report template contains an important section at the end which allows each individual member of the overall diligence effort to add their "bottom line." For example, they might write "I am really impressed with this team and I am planning to invest" or "I think there is a market here but it will cost more than the team thinks so I am not going to invest at this time." We look for as much participation in that section as we can get, and not surprisingly, it is one of the most useful and appreciated sections of our reports.

Q

What happens to the report when it is done?

We "publish" it out to the full Launchpad investor network in connection with a termsheet and a request for soft-circles. And we archive a copy of it on our organization's internal website for future reference.

> Diligence is never done, but it does approach a point of diminishing marginal returns pretty quickly. At some point additional work is not going to bring new insights or further de-risk the investment.

Q

How about all the ancillary materials collected in the dropbox folder?

We circulate the formal items like appendices with the final report, but we put the remaining secondary materials and working papers in an archive and store it for 18 months. Start-ups and their markets move so quickly that there is really very little benefit to lots of old research materials and notes. We like to let the final report speak for itself, but we view the rest of the materials as very perishable and we delete it after 18 months, and usually the company has raised another round by then anyway.

Chapter 26

Good To Go: When You Have Enough to Move Forward

There are a million reasons not to invest in any given startup. Even in the best case, there will be unanswered questions, missing pieces, missing team members, projected losses and uncertainty all around. The diligence process tends to document all of the warts in one place. You would think a compilation of those warts would be the death knell - the final nail in the coffin.

So why do people invest in startups? Because of their potential, and because investors have the experience and necessary framework to put all those risks and uncertainties into the proper perspective. At the earliest stages, ALL startups have problems. The question each investor has to ask is whether those problems are insurmountable.

> At the earliest stages, ALL startups have problems. The question each investor has to ask is whether those problems are insurmountable.

Through the years, Ham has evaluated hundreds of companies, and ultimately, invested in over 50 of these businesses. At Launchpad, he established a process that helps determine whether it makes sense to move forward and make an investment. So let's see what he recommends to investors as they go through this very same challenge.

Q

Ham, what do you do to place some standard procedures into your process of evaluating companies before making an investment?

First of all, there are three very important components in our diligence process. We find that it is extremely helpful in the early days of a diligence project to outline the following three items:

- **Identify Key Risks** - After listening to the entrepreneur's presentation, we caucus to discuss first impressions and immediate top of mind questions and concerns. From that we are able to distill it down and pull together a list of 3 or 4 critical areas that need further examination. The answers to the key questions help us identify the areas of solid ground as well as the key risks that will need to be addressed for the company to achieve a successful exit for the investors.

- **Develop the Investment Thesis** - Ultimately when you are forming an investment thesis, you are building a model or likely scenario in your head. An important filter that can help when assessing potential investment opportunities is sometimes defined as the Three P's: Potential, Probability and Period. For the sake of completeness, we cross-check against our due diligence checklist when forming these questions. But, to keep the process efficient and focused, our diligence team members work together to distill the list of key questions we are really trying to answer and disregard questions which will not add value in a given situation. The answers to the key questions help us identify the areas of solid ground as well.

- **Acknowledge What Needs to Be Believed** - Once we have a handle on the key risks, and we have built an investment thesis, we need to synthesize them into a workable company hypothesis. The best way to keep yourself honest when

doing this is to take the trouble to acknowledge and actually list "what needs to be believed" for the investment to make sense. Thus, when we get to the final stage of our due diligence effort, and we write up our very brief report, we make sure we know and prominently document right at the beginning "What Needs to Be Believed" or WNTBB. If an investor just cannot get comfortable that something on the WNTTB list will come true, then maybe this deal is not for them.

Q

What are the key things you look for in deciding whether there is enough positives to go forward?

First off, I expect to see enthusiasm is mounting for the company, amongst the team. Each of the sub-teams should be coming back with positive results from their research. It's also important that the founders show the following key characteristics while we work with them: high integrity, a straight-forward style, passion about the

201

opportunity, responsiveness in communications, accuracy in information supplied, transparency, cooperation, coachability, and engagement.

> When we get to the final stage of our due diligence effort, and we write up our very brief report, we make sure we know and prominently document right at the beginning "What Needs to Be Believed."

Furthermore, we like to see the company's business continue to progress during diligence. We aren't expecting miracles during this relatively short time period, but we do expect to see some positive movement. We know diligence takes a ton of time, but the team needs to show they can juggle, delegate and prioritize. They cannot let the

business completely go on pause during fundraising.

Finally, as we evaluate demand for the company's product, we expect the customer calls to go extremely well.

Q

When you say "enthusiasm is mounting" does it have to be universal enthusiasm, a majority, or is a minority enough?

The answer to this question depends on your organization. Do you require that all investment decisions are made by 100% of your investors, a majority of your investors, or is a minority good enough? At Launchpad, a minority of investors is enough for us to proceed. So our view is that it does not have to be universal.

For Launchpad, the tricky situations are the divided due diligence teams. If no one intends to invest, it's an easy decision. And, the same is true if everyone likes the company. But when the team is divided it is complicated. You need to look at what your experts think about the key risks in each of their areas. Are there any show stoppers that conflict with your investment thesis and WNTBB? As long as there is no third rail issue, such as a lack of integrity, our approach is to get all the perspectives documented in the report, consider whether the issue merits being on the list of WNTBB items. And assuming it still represents a legitimate investment opportunity, we circulate the report and let individuals decide based on their own personal risk profile.

Q

Aren't the founders exhausted and annoyed at this point in the process? How responsive, engaged, and enthusiastic can you reasonably expect them to be well into a diligence effort?

There's an old joke that goes something like: "An entrepreneur will spend 100% of their time fundraising for their business and the other 100% of their time running the business." If the fundraising process drags on for months and months, it will have a serious negative impact on the CEO. So, it's important that the deal lead set realistic expectations with the entrepreneur. It's important that the entrepreneur try to be responsive and keep the process moving fast. And, it's important that the deal lead be aware of the entrepreneur's need to operate their business at the same time they are supporting the diligence effort.

With that said, the CEO and her team can feel the momentum build as you near a final decision. They are learning more about their business from a well-run diligence process. So while they are tired, they should also be "smelling the oats in the barn" and having great feedback they are eager to test with the money invested in the round.

> It's important that the deal lead be aware of the entrepreneur's need to operate their business at the same time they are supporting the diligence effort.

Q

Why is it important for outside investors to start showing interest at this point?

At Launchpad, we like to lead the deals we are involved in, and we also like to have co-investors involved as an additional source of capital, both in the present and down the road for that company. It's pretty typical that co-investors look to the deal lead to do the heavy lifting on due diligence along with negotiating the investment terms with the company. So we look for a certain level of outside interest as a good litmus test of whether others will be interested and how big an investment syndicate might be possible.

Chapter 27

Let's Make a Deal: Negotiating Terms

Imagine you've always wanted to own a second home, but weren't sure you should buy one. You hem and haw and agonize about the decision, but then one day you finally decide to go for it. There is a brief moment of joy and excitement, but it is quickly followed by a great soberness as the reality sets in. You will have to figure out what to pay for it, get the purchase and sale done, maybe arrange all the paperwork for a mortgage, and find some way to care for it and maintain it in the off-season. This mental process is a lot like what you go through when you decide the diligence on a company is positive enough. At first you are like "OK, let's do this!" and then you realize you've got to set terms, actually make the deal happen, and live with the downstream consequences.

As a deal lead, once you conclude that there is enough of an opportunity to merit potential investment, and around the time you start drafting the final report, you can push through the temporary euphoria and begin negotiating the termsheet. In some cases this will be driven entirely by the deal lead, while in investor networks with dedicated management, it might be led by a manager with the involvement of the deal lead. In either case, it is a vitally important role which is informed by the learnings of the diligence process.

Start-ups have a lot of risk, and the diligence process is really about documenting those risks so that investors can make informed decisions. As we've pointed out in our eBook on Due Diligence, you are not looking for a deal with no risk. You are looking for a situation where you know roughly what you are getting yourself into. (Kind of like the house inspection and budgeting process for that second home!) A termsheet negotiation is about acknowledging all those risks and allocating them between the two sides of a deal. So, it is natural

that the negotiation would be informed by the learnings of the diligence process.

Christopher spent the majority of his career in roles where negotiation was a key part of his responsibilities. And a lot of that time has been spent in early stage investing. So let's put him on the spot to see how he thinks about it.

Q

Christopher, how do you approach the negotiation process when you are leading a deal?

My approach reflects the fact that I lead a large network of investors and tend to be working with really terrific deal leads. I will almost always set myself up to serve as the point person for the negotiation for four reasons:

- It's a huge convenience if the process is led by someone who does a lot of these and is very facile with the terms and terminology and can write a termsheet himself.

- You need someone who has a good sense of what's market and what terms will be acceptable to the investors in the deal.

- It's important to have someone in the discussion who is willing to be be the "bad cop" and hold firm on key terms, like valuation, and not be swayed by pressure or worried about the working relationship with the entrepreneur.

- You want to protect the person who is going to join the board and work closely with the CEO from having to be the heavy in the negotiation.

Q

What is your starting point for the process?

It is important to keep in mind your role in the big picture financing life-cycle of the company. Some inexperienced investors might come into this situation with a scorched earth approach, looking to drive the best possible bargain and the toughest possible terms for

themselves. The problem with that approach is two-fold:

- The toughest set of terms is not necessarily the best bargain for investors.

- The working relationship with the team can affect your outcome and returns as much as the deal terms.

> Start-ups have a lot of risk, and the diligence process is really about documenting those risks so that investors can make informed decisions.

If you go in looking to ram a greedy set of terms through, not only will you potentially cause mistrust and harm the working relationship with the founders, but you may also saddle the company with terms that make it very hard to raise money in a future financing. Subsequent investors may not want to put money into a deal with ridiculous terms for prior investors, or they may insist on the same terms for themselves. Your job as the architect of the first termsheet with the company is not to drive the most aggressive bargain. It is to come up with an acceptable set of terms that is as "vanilla" as it can possibly be. Once you are an investor, you don't want any wrinkles or friction, particularly of your own making, to cause issues with bringing in subsequent financing.

So with that philosophy in mind, I always start off with a standard set of template terms that our investors, lawyers and syndicate partners are used to, and then tweak them and customize them for the specific deal situation. Usually, it is just a handful of routine terms which need tweaking, but other times special issues in the diligence or special aspects of the company's situation require heavier customization. Once I have a draft termsheet to propose, I need to get it in front of the company for reaction.

At this juncture I have a choice. There are two ways to go about forming a termsheet:

- Before sending it, you can walk the entrepreneurs through the concepts and your thoughts on each key term, or

- You can send them a proposed draft termsheet.

I generally base my approach on the sophistication level of the founding team. If they are very experienced and familiar with early stage investing terms, I will generally just prepare a draft termsheet and send it to them. But if they are newer to the whole investment process, then some context and education and perspective might help them better understand the termsheet and react to it more constructively. In this case, I will generally have a conversation and explain the various issues and where I am coming from on each point before sending it over. That way they know roughly what to expect and are not surprised by the harsh black and white of the terms on paper.

> Governance is a very important part of all our deals. In addition to financial capital, we invest a fair amount of human capital into our deals. In most cases, the deal lead will take either a board seat or board observer seat with the company.

It might sound patronizing at first blush, but the reality is that education is a huge part of the early stage negotiation process. Active investors negotiate termsheets all the time and are very comfortable with the concepts. But entrepreneurs have a lot of anxiety and uncertainty, as well as a lot of hot button issues. So it can be really helpful to take the time to explain the logic behind key terms.

Q

What areas merit special attention?

There are a great number of sticky issues in termsheets, but when I am starting a negotiation, most of my thinking and effort goes into:

- Figuring out the right valuation,

- Making sure the option pool is the right size,

- Considering how to construct the board,

- Determining how to structure the founder vesting terms,

- Sizing of the round and the minimum needed to close, and

- Deciding how to structure the liquidation preference.

Vesting for founders and early employees is very important in early stage deals. There is nothing worse than a co-founder of a company owning 20% of the company's stock after working for the company for a year or two. You want all key employees to have two or three years of vesting left, even if they have been involved with the company for quite some time. This may require a restructuring of the cap table.

Governance is a very important part of all our deals. In addition to financial capital, we invest a fair amount of human capital into our deals. In most cases, the deal lead will take either a board seat or board observer seat with the company. This is a key role and requires a fair amount of the deal lead's time over the years when we are active with the portfolio company. For early stage deals, we do not expect to control the board, but we will have a strong voice.

Pre-existing investors are also an area needing attention. One goal of completing a financing is often to clean up the balance sheet, and we need to be certain that any convertible bridge debt is brought over to the equity side of the ledger. In negotiating the termsheet, we need to be mindful of the thresholds and discounts applicable to any outstanding convertible bridge debt. Often upon conversion, bridge debt will entitle holders to a discount off the purchase price in an early stage round, and will require that such round be of a specific size before conversion is mandatory. These terms can be and often are negotiated as part of a round of financing. We need to consider what leverage might exist, in any given situation, before taking the terms of existing convertible debt at face value.

Because securing an exit is important, but can sometimes be at odds with the founders of the company or other legacy stockholders, we require drag along rights. These require all stockholders to approve or otherwise agree to sell their equity in a transaction receiving the affirmative vote of a majority or two-thirds of the shareholders. This becomes an important tool to prevent minority shareholders from threatening to exercise dissenters' rights in a prospective deal or otherwise seeking to gain leverage in an exit transaction by signaling that they will not proceed.

Another important right to secure for our investors is the right to participate in future rounds of financing – sometimes called pre-emptive rights or rights of first refusal. These rights entitle investors in the angel round to participate in any future financings of the company up to their pro rata share of the financing in order to maintain their percentage interest.

Sometimes a company will seek to include a pay-to-play provision that requires investors to exercise this right upon each future financing or otherwise lose pre-emptive rights altogether.

And finally, a key toggle point in any angel financing is whether we will be seeking a straight liquidation preference or a participating preferred structure. Upon a liquidation or sale of the company, a straight liquidation preference entitles the holder to receive either their investment back as a priority to the common stock (and any junior classes of preferred stock) or that which they would otherwise have received had they converted into common stock prior to the transaction. Participating preferred gives the holder the benefit of both worlds: a priority payment equal to the amount invested plus a pro rata amount of any remaining value.

Weak liquidation preferences may not be attractive to investors because they feel they are not being adequately compensated for the early risk they are taking. But overly generous liquidation preferences can turn off later investors or contribute to a massive preference stack that greatly diminishes the early investors returns in weaker exits.

All in all, there are a lot of issues to consider, and getting a termsheet that is going to work for a large investor base can be a pretty tricky process!

So, do you always prepare the first draft?

Yes, it is traditional for investors to prepare the first draft of the termsheet and get it over to the company. That is certainly my strong preference, because if the company does the first draft there are usually a lot of things missing and a lot of wacky off-market terms. When I am drafting and thinking about the termsheet, I will involve the deal lead in the process, if he/she wants to be involved.

> Your job as the architect of the first termsheet with the company is not to drive the most aggressive bargain. It is to come up with an acceptable set of terms that is as "vanilla" as it can possibly be. Once you are an investor, you don't want any wrinkles or friction, particularly of your own making, to cause issues with bringing in subsequent financing.

Q

Do you deliver it in person and sit right down and negotiate?

No. As noted above, I will sometimes talk with the CEO before sending it over. But once I send it, I recognize that companies generally need time to confer with their attorney before responding. So a redline of their thoughts and issues is generally a good next step before sitting down.

Q

How long does that take and what else is going on at that point?

In the background, the deal lead is typically marshaling his or her troops to finish the diligence report, and I am simultaneously giving some thought to issues like potential board and observer appointees and what the best syndication strategy might be.

Q

What happens next?

Once I have comments back from the company we try to hash out an agreement. The goal is to get a mutually acceptable termsheet done right at the same time the final draft of the diligence report is finished. Once the termsheet is done and signed, we publish the diligence report and the termsheet to our investors and begin to syndicate the round.

Chapter 28

Cutting Bait:
When To Walk Away

If one of the trickiest parts of due diligence is knowing when to press ahead in the face of mounting concerns, surely the other tricky part is knowing when to suspend your efforts. The former is a challenge of overcoming inertia and uncertainty, and the latter is a challenge of overcoming momentum.

We talked about the importance of suspending final judgement in the early stages while you gather information, and we also talked about the role of natural "circuit breakers" in the process to make sure you don't end up with a small minority of enthusiastic people leading to a bad case of deal momentum.

In a realm where every deal is imperfect, how do you tell when something is just too flawed to accept? Ham has been in this position many times before, so let's see what insights he can offer.

Q

Ham, what are some of the signs that it might be time to bail?

Give me a few hours and I can describe dozens of signs. Over the past 15 years, I've run into many different situations, but I would have to say the following five issues are the most common:

- **Entrepreneur Integrity**: If you suspect that you are running into

ANY issues around the integrity of the entrepreneur, you are done.

- **Big Surprises**: Some of the surprises I have run into over the years include:

  - Finding out the company has a lot of debt they need to pay off,

  - A key founder quits during diligence,

  - The company doesn't have ownership of vital Intellectual Property.

- **Big Shortcomings**: These situations can be a bit more challenging to determine whether you are looking at something fatal or not. It takes a bit more judgement on the part of the diligence team. Examples might include:

  - The size of the market opportunity is not large enough,

  - The company requires too much capital to make this a slam-dunk win for early investors,

- Customer reference checks come back lukewarm.

- **Loss of Enthusiasm and Interest**: This is the case where you have lost all momentum within the diligence team and you won't be able to raise any significant capital for the company. You might have one or two interested investors, but that's not enough to properly support the company with this round of financing.

- **Company Intransigence**: There are times when the CEO is just not willing to compromise. For example, you start the negotiation of a termsheet, and your position and the CEO's position are too far apart. If that happens, it can be very difficult to come up with a deal that's seen as fair for both sides.

Q

When you talk about integrity issues, what are you referring to? Is it always obvious?

When we look to make an investment in a company, the most important factor in our decision is the quality of the team. The key characteristic we look for in the CEO is integrity. That character trait might sound obvious, but I feel it's very important to be on alert for trust issues when you are interacting with an entrepreneur. From the initial meeting with the company, during the due diligence process, and finally while negotiating the deal, I want to make sure the CEO is being honest and negotiates in a fair manner. If I sense any duplicity at this early a stage, I can be sure that things will only get worse as the company progresses from the honeymoon phase through the challenges faced by all startups.

Q

Why do you cite surprises as a reason to give up? Aren't surprises an expected outcome of a fact-gathering exercise?

There are surprises and then there are SURPRISES! When you first start diligence, you should expect to learn things about a company that you didn't expect. Examples might include the product is really buggy, or the first few customers paid almost nothing for the product. These are the types of "warts" you expect to uncover in almost all early stage companies.

As you might surmise from the examples I gave in the list above (i.e. debt, loss of a key founder, lack of IP ownership), I am talking about surprises that indicate the CEO is hiding something from us or ignorant about what makes a company valuable. With debt, it could mean the CEO isn't being truthful about the company's financial position or is too financially unsophisticated to understand why that is a big problem. The loss of a key founder might speak to the

CEO's ability to build a great team. And finally, with lack of IP ownership, the CEO doesn't realize the importance of IP to a future acquirer.

> When we look to make an investment in a company, the most important factor in our decision is the quality of the team. The key characteristic we look for in the CEO is integrity.

You talk about fatal shortcomings. Is one section, one area of weakness, enough to tank an entire due diligence process? If not, what does it take? If most startups need work in most areas, aren't all of the sections going to be a little weak?

It's important to distinguish between areas where a bit more work or experimentation is needed by the company versus true fatal flaws that will be very difficult, if not impossible to correct. The examples that I cite above (i.e. market size and capital requirements) are very tough to overcome.

Let me be a bit more concrete. Let's look at Market Size. If you add up all the potential customers for the product and multiply by how much they will pay for the product, and you end up with a $5M market opportunity, the company shouldn't be taking in any outside investors. It might still be a nice little business, but not one that can work with outside investors. The CEO is better off bootstrapping the business.

Here's another example. Suppose the company has a product that needs a lot of explanation before the customer will buy, and therefore, they need to build a direct sales organization. Furthermore, their average customer spends $1,000 per year for this product. Unfortunately, their go-to-market strategy has a fatal flaw. A direct sales organization is too expensive given the price of their product.

All that said, sometimes the fatal flaw is not so fatal after all. In some cases, it's the ignorance of the CEO that gives the appearance of a fatal flaw. For example, maybe the company I described above doesn't need a direct sales organization. Perhaps a member of the diligence team can show the CEO how to sell the product using a strategy that is significantly less expensive for the company. That's how a great investor adds value by applying their financial capital and human capital to help the company.

And, to answer your last question, there will be weakness in at least one section of the diligence report and probably multiple sections. That's just the nature of seed stage investing. You can't expect perfection when a company is at such an early stage!

Q

How do you interpret team interest issues if the deal lead is always called on to be a cheerleader to some extent?

In the majority of diligence projects, the deal lead does play the role of cheerleader. The deal lead wants and expects the other diligence team members to be excited about the company. But, to be fair, not everyone has an upbeat personality. And, you can't expect every member of the diligence team to remain enthusiastic during the entire diligence process. Individual risk tolerances and interest areas differ, so some will always want to get off the merry-go-round before others.

So how do you gauge whether interest in the company is high enough to justify continuing the diligence process? We use the interim call as an opportunity to do a roll call or "show of hands". We also monitor the one-on-one interactions we have with the diligence team members. We pay attention to the level of expertise of the different team members. If your experts are bailing early, that is a bigger signal than if a few generalists wander off the reservation. And finally, we do our own gut check to see if we are just "not feeling it" and whether we think the larger investor group will be interested.

Making sure that the company is properly financed is one of a CEO's top priorities, and so being busy is not an excuse for lack of responsiveness. Ultimately, you are looking to build a great partnership. If you feel that it's a one way street, you will need to either fix the problem or move on to your next investment.

Q

How do you define "company intransigence"? What is the difference between being busy and unresponsive?

At the end of the day, once you have the official closing on your investment, you expect to have established a strong partnership with the CEO. The investors and company management are now on this journey together. And, a long journey it will be. Most successful early stage companies can take 7-10 years before they reach an exit. If you run into "company intransigence" during diligence, you are setting yourself up for a very long and rocky marriage!

So, how do I define intransigence in this situation? I can think of four areas where the CEO has serious shortcomings:

- **Responsiveness**: It takes many days to get replies to our email requests,

- **Cooperation**: Not helpful in setting up customer calls, management meetings,

- **Coachability**: Not willing to take guidance from experienced business people, and

- **Flexibility**: Difficult to pin down for meetings and phone calls.

You should expect that a CEO has much work to do and that your requests are not the only things on her plate. Remember, she has a business to run in addition to putting time into fundraising. That said, making sure that the company is properly financed is one of a CEO's top priorities, and so being busy is not an excuse for lack of responsiveness. Ultimately, you are looking to build a great partnership. If you feel that it's a one way street, you will need to either fix the problem or move on to your next investment.

221

Appendix

At Launchpad Venture Group, we provide our investors with a series of templates to help facilitate the due diligence process. In this appendix, we include example templates that we use on a regular basis.

- **Deep Dive Meeting Notes Template**: This template records key items from the initial company presentation and from our deep dive meetings. It helps organize our due diligence efforts.

- **Due Diligence Report**: This template is designed to result in a short, readable due diligence report. Our goal at Launchpad is to provide our investors with a 2 to 4 page summary report that is readable and comprehensive. It covers all the main areas in diligence and provides the author(s) with a structured approach.

- **Due Diligence Checklist**: After reading this book, you might feel overwhelmed by all the different aspects in due diligence. The Due Diligence Checklist is designed as a quick reference guide to help steer you through the various aspects of diligence.

- **Customer Reference Check Questionnaire**: At the core of this questionnaire are a series of questions that will help you distinguish whether the company is selling aspirin, oxygen or jewelry. And, you can find out a bit more about the size of the potential market opportunity.

- **Management Assessment Questionnaire**: This questionnaire is designed to get the story behind the CEO and his/her team. If you are able to make enough reference calls, you should be able to find similarities and differences to help you paint a pretty good picture of the team you are investing in.

Deep Dive Meeting Notes Template

This template records key items from the initial company presentation and from our deep dive meetings. It helps organize our due diligence efforts.

Deep Dive Meeting with {NewCo}   {Date}, {Location}

Company Attendees

Name	Role	Name	Role
{Name 1}	CEO	{Name 2}	CTO
{Name 3}	??	{Name 4}	??

Investor Attendees

Name	Name	Name	Name
{Name 1}	{Name 2}		

Additional Investors Originally Expressing Interest but Not in Attendance

Name	Name	Name	Name
{Name 1}	{Name 2}		

Contents Of This Document:

1. Summary of Next Steps after the Deep Dive Meeting
2. Key Themes Raised at Original Pitch Meeting
3. Post-Pitch Investor Questions & Company's Written Answers
4. Q&A Notes from the Deep Dive Meeting
5. Materials from Deep Dive Meeting (These are provided by NewCo)

Summary of Post Deep Dive Next Steps:

{Provide a short two or three sentence summary of the outcome of the meeting. For example: "This was a well-attended and productive discussion. We covered everything we wanted to cover except the financial projections. Coming out of the meeting there was near universal enthusiasm for moving forward, so we decided to form a team and progress to due diligence." }

(Use this table to record team assignments. Subject areas can be customized or combined as needed. The "Notes" column may not be needed in each case, but it is the place to record a contact, expert, question, special task, possible additional volunteer, time constraint or other item of interest relating to the topic assignment.)

Subject	Volunteers	Notes	Subject	Volunteers	Notes
Diligence Team Lead	Name	notes	Market Size, Market Opportunity, Regulatory	Name	notes
Customers	Name	notes	Financial Model	Name	notes
Leadership Assessment	Name	notes	Valuation & Funding Strategy	Name	notes
Tech & IP / Competition	Name	notes	Investors / Deal Terms	Name	notes
Sales & Marketing	Name	notes	Exit Strategy / Payoff	Name	notes

*Assistance requested, but not yet confirmed.

Agenda & Themes Raised at the Original Pitch Meeting:

(This section is where you organize the notes and reactions from the investor pitch. Positives are optional, but they are very helpful to teams looking to understand which parts of the pitch worked. The "Key Concerns" box is where you try and condense and organize the investor concerns, questions and feedback into a more manageable number of "themes" or groupings and use that to organize the deep dive meeting. A deep dive meeting can really only cover 2-4 topics in any depth, so it is important to boil it down into themes.)

Positives Noted	Key Concerns / Themes to Organize Deep Dive
Item 1	Issue One (50 minutes of deep dive time)
Item 2	.
.	.
.	.
.	Issue Two (30 minutes of deep dive time)
	.
	.
	Issue Three (15 minutes of deep dive time)
	.
	.
	.

Discussion Notes:

[Insert summary of meeting intros and other notes relating to the meeting kick off here in this intro paragraph. For example, if the meeting started with a demo, the highlights can be summarized here.]

[The remainder of the notes just attempt to capture the flow of the meeting. Q&A format works well because it allows for fast and efficient note taking and also helps capture the quality of the give and take. It is hard to get it perfect working live in the meeting, but if you capture the gist of the question and a few notes on the answer, you can easily go back and flesh it out when editing it prior to distribution.]

Q: Example investor question?

A: Example notes on entrepreneur answer.

Q: Example investor question?

A: Example notes on entrepreneur answer.

Q: Example investor question?

A: Example notes on entrepreneur answer.

Q:

A:

Q:

A:

Factual Questions The Company Answered in Writing Prior to Deep Dive:

Typically provided as a set of slides or a document with answers to questions sent in advance of the deep dive meeting.

Due Diligence Report

This template is designed to result in a short, readable due diligence report. Our goal at Launchpad is to provide our investors with a 2 to 4 page summary report that is readable and comprehensive. It covers all the main areas in diligence and provides the author(s) with a structured approach.

Company: {Company Name}

CEO: {CEO Name}

Report Date: {Date}

Company Description:

{insert 1-2 paragraph summary description of company here}

Due Diligence Assessment:

{This section is the heart of the due diligence report. For each topic, we provide you with example questions that make for appropriate areas to discuss in the remarks column. This report template is deliberately designed as a table to force the authors to be concise. It's important to be succinct in your diligence findings summary. Otherwise, you will end up with a long report that investors won't read through, thus defeating the purpose of the report. If you have important detail or documents that you feel must be included in your findings, you can make them into appendices and refer to them in the report, but can be a slippery slope toward an excessively long package. A better approach is to keep primary research materials and memos in a cloud folder you can make available to the minority of investors who want more detail.}

Topic	Rating	Remarks
Investment Thesis		
What Needs To Be Believed (WNTBB)		
Failure Risk		
Leadership Assessment		
Technology, IP and Product Roadmap		
Customer Need and Go-To-Market Plan		
Uniqueness and Competition		
Market Size and Market Opportunity		
Financial Projections and Funding Strategy		
Exit Strategy		
Deal Terms and Payoff		

Note: See page 237 for the Rating Key and pages 238-242 for details on what remarks to supply in each of these sections.

Individual Assessments:

{This section of the report is designed to allow each member of the due diligence team to provide some short feedback on their personal opinion of the investment opportunity. You shouldn't expect everyone's assessment to be positive. In fact, it's important to have at least one or two dissenting opinions to add balance to the report. And, make sure to ask for succinct summary comments. It is especially helpful if each commenter ends their comments with a note about whether they plan to invest and why/why not.}

Team Member	Rating	Summary Remarks
{Name 1}		
{Name 2}		
{Name 3}		

Key

(++) = Very Positive (+) = Positive (0) = Neutral

(–) = Negative but issues can be overcome

(/)Very Negative, issues cannot be overcome

Investment Thesis: This section is where you explain the overall logic of the investment and characterize how it is that investors will make money. Questions you may want to cover here include:

- Is this a billion dollar IPO opportunity or is it more likely to be acquired for under $50M? Or something in between?

- Are there limited number of risks that can be mitigated or is this a moonshot deal with big risk and potentially big reward?

- Will it take 10 years to complete the product and get FDA approval, or could this company be acquired in the first couple of years by a big competitor?

What Needs to Be Believed (WNTBB): This section is where you boil down all of the key risks that need to be assumed in order to invest (see companion eBook for more detail). If an investor cannot make peace with or cannot believe an item on this list can be overcome, she should not invest. Example WNTBBs might include:

- That this market can be disrupted.

- That enough customers will find this essential at this price point.

- That the company will be successful in transitioning from current niche to mainstream.

- That the company can build out a successful go to market plan and demonstrate traction on this round size.

- That this management team can scale to pull this off.

- That the company can achieve market share before the large competitors crowd them out.

Failure Risk: This section is where you talk about the main weaknesses in the plan and the degree to which they are mitigated. If this company fails is it likely for lack of capitalization, inability to make the technology work, competition?

Leadership Assessment: This section is where you discuss your assessment of the management team. Questions you may want to cover here include:

- Does the CEO possess the experience and leadership abilities to succeed?
- Do they have skills for where they are going, as opposed to where they have been?
- Do the CEO and team have a proven track record?
- Does the team possess the appropriate balance of experience and skill sets?
- Are the board members and advisors suitable and committed?
- What key hires are needed to address gaps?

Technology, IP and Product Roadmap: This section is where you discuss your assessment of the technology and technology risk as well as the IP situation. Questions you may want to cover here include:

- Is the technical team qualified and experienced?
- How strong are the technology and IP positions?
- Is there a product roadmap and is it achievable?
- What are the remaining risks related to technology, IP and product roadmap?
- Are their superior technologies on the near term horizon?

Customer Need and Go-To-Market Plan: This section is where you discuss your assessment of the plan to take the product to market. Questions you may want to cover here include:

- Is the GTM plan sufficiently detailed?

- Are the assumptions, including required level of sales spend and time lines reasonable?

- Is the sales pipeline adequate, and are key metrics for adoption rate, conversion rates, etc. conservative?

- Do customers confirm the need and likely adoption rates?

- Beyond verifying some demand, do we understand the customers buying priorities? Is this Oxygen, Aspirin or Jewelry?

- What are the major risks in marketing awareness, customer adoption rates and sales cycle?

Uniqueness and Competition: This section is where you discuss your assessment of the overall competitiveness and defensibility of the offering. Questions you may want to cover here include:

- Is the company well positioned with respect to current and likely future competitors?

- Is the founding team well-informed about their market and industry? Do they have a good competitive sense, or are they unaware of key issues?

- What are the major risks in marketing awareness, customer adoption rates and sales cycle?

Market Size and Market Opportunity: This section is where you discuss your assessment of the actual addressable market. Questions you may want to cover here include:

- Are the top-down and bottoms-up market estimates consistent and attractive?

- Are the market share projections reasonable?

- What are the remaining risks in market development?

Financial Projections and Funding Strategy: This section is where you discuss your assessment of the financial plan and capital raising strategy. Questions you may want to cover here include:

- Does the balance sheet make sense, and are there any showstopper issues?

- Are the financial projections reasonable and conservative in light of past performance?

- What are the implications of variances in key assumptions?

- Is the future financing risk manageable?

- What are remaining financial risks?

- Are the assumptions about scaling expense (e.g. G&A, etc.) reasonable, or is the model unrealistic?

Exit Strategy: This section is where you discuss your assessment of the likely exit opportunities. Questions you may want to cover here include:

- Is there alignment with the CEO and team on exit goals?

- Is the exit strategy reasonable?

- Is the assumed timeline reasonable?

- What exit multiples can be predicted under representative scenarios?

- Does the CEO know people in the industry? Is he/she a networker who will make the relationships and do the thought-leadership necessary to get a buyer interested?

Deal Terms and Payoff: This section is where you summarize the relationship between the deal terms in the termsheet and the expected investor return. Questions you may want to cover here include:

- Is this a low valuation, high risk deal, or a high valuation, low risk deal?

- Does the termsheet include specific terms intended to protect this round of investors?

- Can you show the desired return multiple based on exit multiples for comparable companies?

Due Diligence Checklist

This checklist is designed to be appropriate for early stage investments. The "Information Request" and "Tasks" columns list those items and tasks, respectively, that are generally required, at a minimum, to complete diligence. The "Key Questions" column is representative of typical questions the diligence effort should address. The information request, tasks, and key questions should all be reviewed and revised, as needed, for the particular situation. The "Summary Points" column may be used by the team to summarize the answers to key questions in preparation for drafting the diligence report. Thank you to Launchpad member Gail Greenwald for her help developing this checklist.

Leadership Assessment

Information Request	Tasks	Key Questions
Resumes for key leadership team members	Review resumes	Does the CEO possess the experience and leadership abilities to succeed?
Professional references for key team members	Interview references (see interview guidelines)	Do they have skills for where they are going, as opposed to where they have been?
Resumes and contact info for board members and advisors	Gather additional information from network as available (asking around, checking LinkedIn - anything to find blind reference checks)	Do the CEO and team have a proven track record?
	Assign team member(s) to spend time with CEO	Does the team possess the appropriate balance of experience and skill sets?
	Assess CEO and team for leadership, integrity, track record, required competencies	Are the board members and advisors suitable and committed?
	Assess suitability and commitment of board members and advisors	What key hires are needed to address gaps?

Technology, IP and Product Roadmap

Information Request	Tasks	Key Questions
Descriptions of technology and product	Review information and meet with technical team	Is the technical team qualified and experienced?
Relevant technical publications	Assess critical technologies, tool choices, software architecture choices, scalability of solution	How strong are the technology and IP positions?
Patents and patent applications	Assess IP defensibility	Is the product roadmap achievable?
Related IP info (defense: Freedom to Operate (FTO)?, offense: enforceability?)	Conduct additional secondary research as needed	What are the remaining risks related to technology, IP and product roadmap?
Product roadmap with key milestones	Conduct additional expert interviews if needed	Are their superior technologies on the near term horizon?
Competing technologies and commercialization status	Assess remaining technical risk, IP defensibility, competitive technical position	

Regulatory Strategy

Information Request	Tasks	Key Questions
Regulatory strategy, if relevant	Review regulatory strategy	Is the regulatory strategy well thought through and feasible?
Status of dialogue with regulatory authorities and/or consultants, copies of relevant communications	Interview regulatory experts	Are the company's financial resources sufficient to implement the regulatory plan?
	Assess comparable regulatory pathways for other products as appropriate	Are assumptions about partners/acquirers' roles in the regulatory plan reasonable?
	Assess regulatory climate	What are the remaining regulatory risks?

Customer Need and Go-to-Market Plan

Information Request	Tasks	Key Questions
Go-to-market plan with key milestones and granular detail on sales approach	Review information and meet with marketing and sales team	Is the GTM plan reasonable?
Partner identification and relationship status	Interview customers, partners, prospects as appropriate	Is the sales pipeline adequate, and are key metrics for adoption rate, conversion rates, etc. conservative?
Sales pipeline by stage, factored to be truly realistic and achievable	Gather information on industry comparisons as appropriate	Do customers confirm the need and likely adoption rates?
Any current marketing, joint venture, distribution agreements	Collaborate with financial team to assess revenue and pricing model	Beyond verifying some demand, do we understand the customers buying priorities? Is this Oxygen, Aspirin or Jewelry?
Customer, prospect, and partner references (see guidelines for interviewing customers)		What are the major risks in marketing awareness, customer adoption rates and sales cycle?

Uniqueness and Competition

Information Request	Tasks	Key Questions
List of current and prospective competitors	Gather additional competitive intelligence as needed	Is the company well positioned with respect to current and likely future competitors?
Competitive analysis including market share, relative strengths and weaknesses	Assess competitive environment, competitor positions, barriers to entry	Is the founding team well-informed about their market and industry? Do they have a good competitive sense, or are they unaware of key issues?
		What are the major risks in marketing awareness, customer adoption rates and sales cycle?

Customer Reference Check Questionnaire

At the core of this questionnaire are a series of questions that will help you distinguish whether the company is selling aspirin, oxygen or jewelry. And, you can find out a bit more about the size of the potential market opportunity.

Customer Reference Check Questionnaire

What are the reasons for purchasing company's products/services? What problem does this product/service solve for you?

Is this product a "Need to Have" or a "Nice to Have" for your organization?

What are your expectations / goals for this (e.g. improved revenue, reduced costs, etc.)?

Does the ROI for this product justify the current pricing? Would you expect to pay more or less for the product?

Have you used similar products/services before?

On your list of the top problems in your organization, where does solving this problem fall on your priority list?

Is your company generally an early or late adopter of new solutions?

Which products/services from the company do you use? Do you expect to add additional products/services in the future?

Did you look at any competitive products?

Why did you select company over other competitors?

As a customer/prospect for (company's) products/services, how did your interaction with the company go? Did they meet your expectations?

What is your impression of the company's management team?

Management Assessment Questionnaire

This questionnaire is designed to get the story behind the CEO and his/her team. If you are able to make enough reference calls, you should be able to find similarities and differences to help you paint a pretty good picture of the team you are investing in.

Management Assessment Questionnaire
What are {CEO Name's} strengths?
What are some areas for further development?
What's the best way to tell {CEO Name} something you know he/she doesn't want to hear?
How does {CEO Name} use advisors? Does he/she share everything and ask for reaction, or does he/she just come with specific (e.g. narrow questions / concerns?) How open is he/she to influence from advisors (e.g. investors?)
If {Company Name} were to fail due to leadership, it would be because of what characteristic of {CEO Name}?
Does {CEO Name} show sufficient emotional intelligence to be able to navigate the typical ups and downs of an early stage company?
Do one or more members of the management team have a proven track record and does prior track record include successful exit(s)/returned money to investors?
Does the management team have applicable domain expertise?
Does the management team have complementary skills?

This book is brought to you by the founders of **Seraf.** Seraf is a web-based portfolio management tool for investors in early stage companies. Seraf's intuitive dashboard gives angel investors the power to organize all of their angel activities in one online workspace. With Seraf, investors can see the combined value of their holdings, monitor company progress, analyze key performance metrics, track tax issues, store investment documents in a cloud-based digital locker, and more. Seraf's easy interface enables investors to track their angel portfolios as efficiently as they track their public investments. To learn more, visit **Seraf-Investor.com**.

Hambleton Lord is Co-Founder of Seraf and the Co-Managing Director of Launchpad Venture Group, an angel investment group focused on seed and early-stage investments in technology-oriented companies. Ham has built a personal portfolio of more than 35 early stage investments and is a board member, advisor and mentor to numerous start-ups.

Seraf Co-Founder **Christopher Mirabile** is the Chair of the Angel Capital Association and also Co-Managing Director of Launchpad Venture Group. He has personally invested in over 50 start-up companies and is a limited partner in four specialized angel funds. Christopher is a frequent panelist and speaker on entrepreneurship and angel-related topics and serves as an adjunct lecturer in Entrepreneurship in the MBA program at Babson. Due to their combination of roles as investors, advisors and angel group leaders, Ham and Christopher were named among Xconomy's "Top Angel Investors in New England."